P. J. FEAR.

29

BBC BASIC

R.B. Coats

Principal Lecturer in Computer Studies
Leicester Polytechnic

Edward Arnold (Publishers) Ltd. hereby warrant that this book is in no way
connected with either the BBC or the manufacturers of the computer, Acorn.

Edward Arnold

© R.B. Coats 1983
Reprinted 1983, 1984

First published in Great Britain 1983 by
Edward Arnold (publishers) Ltd, 41 Bedford Square, London WC1B 3DQ

Edward Arnold, 300 North Charles Street, Baltimore, Maryland 21201, U.S.A.

Edward Arnold (Australia) Pty Ltd, 80 Waverley Road, Caulfield East, Victoria 3145, Australia

ISBN 0 7131 3497 6

All rights reserved. No part of this publication may be reproduced, stored in a retrieval system, or transmitted in any form or by any means, electronic, mechanical, photocopying, recording or otherwise, without the prior permission of Edward Arnold (Publishers) Ltd.

Printed in Great Britain by Butler & Tanner Ltd, Frome and London

Preface

This book describes how to program the BBC computer in BASIC. It is written in such a way that young people (aged about 12 and upwards) will be able to use it. Simple examples are used throughout the book; these examples are easy to understand, and require no mathematics. Many of the examples are, in fact, drawn from a school environment, so the book is particularly relevant to schools and colleges.

The book assumes that you have a BBC computer of your own (or have ready access to one), and that you have gained some familiarity with it, to the extent of being able to RUN programs (games, for example), and being able to enter data via the keyboard, as requested by these programs.

Experience has shown that BASIC is best taught by the combination of a book and a computer. The printed page is good at explaining concepts. The computer, on the other hand, is good at testing your understanding of these concepts; it responds quickly, and provides immediate evidence as to whether you have understood. Hence, an essential component of this book are the practical exercises that are to be tried on your computer.

The book is divided into thirty-one Units. Each Unit concentrates on a particular aspect of BASIC, and consists of:

written text, explaining that aspect of BASIC;

practical exercises, testing and reinforcing your understanding;

questions at the end of the Unit, challenging you to apply the knowledge you have just acquired.

The book has three PARTS, each containing a number of Units. At the end of each PART, there is an Example Program. This program uses many of the aspects of BASIC that have been covered in that PART, and is intended to revise these aspects of BASIC in your mind. In addition, these Example Programs demonstrate how larger programs are designed and constructed.

This book places strong emphasis on 'good' programming. Sound programming techniques are taught throughout the book, and all the material has been tested on a BBC computer.

My particular thanks go to Peter Messer for the time and effort he spent reading the manuscript, and for his perceptive comments and constructive criticisms which stimulated many improvements to the book. I am also indebted to Steve Scrivener for his artistic interpretation of the 'shoot-the-letter' program in Unit 27, and to Andrew Parkin for proof-reading the final version of the book.

I wish to thank Leicester Polytechnic for the use of their computer facilities to prepare this book.

Finally, I am very grateful to my wife and children for their encouragement and help, without which this book could not possibly have been written. In particular, I would like to thank David (aged 12) and Martin (aged 9) for acting as guinea pigs for the early chapters of the book, and for their many suggestions which were incorporated into the final version.

March 1983   R.B.Coats

Contents

APPENDICES

1 Introduction

1.1 Using this book

BASIC is a language which was designed to be easy for beginners to learn. Because of its simplicity, it has become widely available, and nearly all computers provide it. The aim of this book is to teach you how to program the BBC computer in BASIC.

The book assumes that you have a BBC computer of your own (or have access to one), and that you have become familiar with using it. Before starting on this book, you should go through the 'WELCOME' package. This explains how to get your computer working, and it also demonstrates many of the things which a computer can do.

This book is organised into Units. Each unit concentrates on a particular aspect of BASIC, and assumes that you understand the previous units. Therefore, the units must be tackled in order. In each unit there are three components:

The written text
describing the particular aspect of BASIC covered in the unit.

Practical exercises
to be carried out on your computer. Learning to program is similar to learning to ride a bicycle – you learn by trying to ride, and not by reading about it. Hence, these exercises are very important, because they reinforce your understanding of the unit.

Questions
at the end of the unit, to challenge you to apply the knowledge that you have just acquired. Answers are provided in Appendix A to SOME of these questions; those with an answer are indicated by an * immediately following the question number.

All the practical exercises and the questions should be completed before going on to the next unit.

1.2 Computers

There are three main parts to a computer.

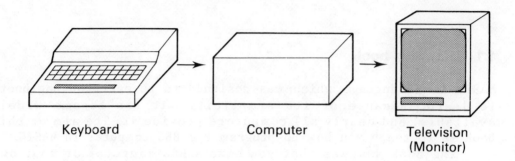

Keyboard   Computer   Television
                                    (Monitor)

1.   The KEYBOARD, which is used to enter information into the
     computer. The information that is entered into a computer is
     called the input.

2.   The COMPUTER itself, which manipulates information. For
     example, it might add two numbers together. Or it might sort
     a list of names into alphabetical order.

3.   The TELEVISION (or MONITOR), which is used to display the
     results produced by the computer. For example, it might show
     the answer obtained from adding the two numbers. Or it might
     display the names in alphabetical order. The information
     that is sent out by the computer to the screen is called the
     output.

You can get the computer to do something by giving it a command.
A command is typed on the keyboard. When you have finished typing
the command, you must always press the RETURN key, to let the
computer know that you are ready for it to obey the command. The
computer will now obey the command, and then wait for you to
enter another command. Normally, the word 'execute' is used to
describe what a computer does with a command, rather than the
word 'obey' ('execute' means 'carry out'). Hence, a computer is
said to execute a command.
     You can tell when the computer is waiting for a command
because it displays a 'prompt' on the screen. The prompt on the
BBC computer is the > character. Pressing the RETURN key causes a
new line to be taken. If you forget to press RETURN, it will be
obvious since you will have two commands on the same line.

PRACTICAL EXERCISES

PRINT is a command. It is used to make the computer display something on the screen.

Type
>   PRINT 2+3   and then press RETURN.

The computer should display 5 on the screen.

Type
>   PRINT 7+4

>   PRINT 27+31

>   PRINT 8-3

>   PRINT 17-5

Did you remember to press the RETURN key each time? Note that '-' is on the same key as '=', and means subtract (take). Check that the computer's answers are correct.

Type
>   PINT 5+4

Note that PRINT has been spelt incorrectly: you missed out the R. Typing mistakes are common, especially for the beginner. Fortunately, there is no harm done. The computer only recognises certain commands, and PINT is not one of them. So it tells you that you have made a mistake.
>   If you realise that you have made a mistake BEFORE you press the RETURN key, then you can correct it. If you press the DELETE key once, the last character you typed is deleted. If you press it again, another character is deleted. And so on.

Type
>   PINT   but don't press the RETURN key.

>   Press DELETE   and the T should disappear.

>   Press DELETE   and the N should disappear.

>   Press DELETE   and the I should disappear.

Now type

        RINT 2+3   and press RETURN.

The command should be executed correctly. From now on, you won't
be reminded to press RETURN after each command. This is something
you will have to remember for yourself.

- -

Type
        CALCULATE 2+3

        DISPLAY 2+3

Although the English looks correct, the computer does not know
the meaning of the words CALCULATE and DISPLAY, and so thinks you
have made a mistake. The computer will only accept words it
knows, and the one for displaying something on the screen is
PRINT.

- -

The computer can also perform multiplication (times) and division
(divides).

Type
        PRINT 2*3

        PRINT 10*10

        PRINT 8/2

        PRINT 10/5

The asterisk (*) tells the computer to do multiplication; the
forward slash (/) tells the computer to do division. Check that
the computer's answers are correct.

- -

This exercise shows the effect of inserting spaces in a command.

Type
        PRINT2*4

        PRINT 2*4

        PRINT 2   *   4

        PRIN T 2*4

All these are valid commands except the last one. Spaces can be inserted between words and numbers, but it is wrong to insert spaces between the letters making up a word: PRIN T is incorrect because of the space between the N and the T.

You should always put a space after a command word. For example:

    PRINT 2/3   is clearer than

    PRINT2/3

It is even more important when dealing with more complicated commands, which we meet in later units:

    IF AGE <18 THEN PRINT "CHILD"   is clearer than

    IFAGE<18THENPRINT"CHILD"

Questions

1. What is meant by the word <u>input</u>? *The information that is entered into a computer.*

2. How do you provide 'input' to your computer? *Keyboard.*

3. What is meant by the word <u>output</u>? *The information that is sent out by the computer to the screen*

4. Where does the 'output' from your computer appear? *screen?*

5. What is a <u>command</u>? *an instruction to the computer to do something.*

6. You have met one command in this unit. What is it? *PRINT*

7. How do you give a command to the computer? *Typing on a keyboard.*

8. What is meant by <u>executing</u> a command? *to carry out a command.*

9. What happens when you press the RETURN key after typing in a command? *a 'prompt' is displayed on the screen.*

10. What happens if you give the computer a command that is spelt incorrectly? *It tells you that you have made a mistake*

11. Work out what the computer will do with these commands.
Write your answers in the 'your answer' column.

command	your answer	computer
PRINT 3+4	3+4 =	
PRINT 8-7		
PRINT 4*3		
PRINT 18/6		
PING 9+7		
PRINT 3 + 4		
CALCULATE 3+4		
PRI NT 3+4		
PRINT 7+3+4		
PRINT 7+3-4		

Now type the commands into the computer, and see if you were
right.

12. How do you correct typing mistakes? Make some deliberate
mistakes, and then practise correcting them.

2 Variables

2.1 Computer memory

A computer has a memory. It stores information in its memory just as you store information in your memory. Information can be both recalled (got back from memory) and remembered (saved in memory for future recall). This unit describes how you can use BASIC to save information in, and recall information from, your computer's memory.

You can think of a computer's memory as being made up of a large number of boxes.

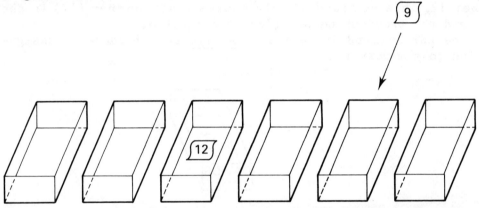

Each box can hold one piece of information. At this stage we will only consider numbers being stored in the boxes, but in later units we will see that other information (this book, for example) can be stored as well. In the diagram above, the third box from the left contains the number 12, and the number 9 is being put into the fifth box.

How does BASIC make use of these boxes? Suppose you want to tell the computer about the age of a boy called DAVID. This can be done by typing the command

    LET DAVIDSAGE=12

The computer will respond to the command as follows:

    a) it selects ONE of its unused memory boxes;
    b) it attaches the name DAVIDSAGE to this box;
    c) finally it stores the number 12 in the box.

The boxes making up a computer's memory are 'electronic boxes' which cannot be seen with your eyes. So how can you be sure that the computer has created a box called DAVIDSAGE? Remembering that the PRINT command causes something to be displayed on the screen, try typing

      LET DAVIDSAGE=12
      PRINT DAVIDSAGE
            12

and see what happens. Success! The computer will display the contents of the named box.

      A name such as DAVIDSAGE is called a <u>variable</u>. It is said to be 'variable' because the contents of its box can be altered. For example, after David's next birthday, you might type

      LET DAVIDSAGE=13

The box for DAVIDSAGE already exists, and it currently holds the number 12. This command simply stores a new number (13) in the box, and the previous number (12) is forgotten.

      The LET command is called an <u>assignment</u>, because it assigns a value to a memory box.

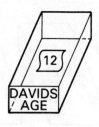

PRACTICAL EXERCISES

- -

Type
      LET MARTINSAGE=9
      PRINT MARTINSAGE
            9

Does the computer do as you expect?

- -

Type

```
LET MARTINSAGE=10
PRINT MARTINSAGE
```
10

The MARTINSAGE memory box should now contain the number 10.

- -

Type

```
PRINT ALISONSAGE
```

The computer should tell you that you have made an error. A memory box called ALISONSAGE can only be created by an assignment such as LET ALISONSAGE=5. Since you haven't typed such a command, the computer doesn't have a box called ALISONSAGE, and therefore it cannot display its contents.

- -

Type

```
PRINT DAVIDSAGE
NEW
PRINT DAVIDSAGE
```

The NEW command tells the computer to forget about all the names that have so far been attached to the boxes, and to start again. You can think of the computer rubbing off the names. Hence, following the NEW command, it doesn't know about DAVIDSAGE and MARTINSAGE, and when you try to use one of these names, the computer tells you that you have made a mistake.

- -

Suppose David is paid pocket money by his parents. Each week he receives five pence for each year of his age. If he is 10, he gets 50 pence per week; if he is 11, he gets 55 pence; and so on.

Type

```
LET DAVIDSAGE=10
PRINT DAVIDSAGE
```
10

| 10 |
| DAVIDSAGE |

The LET command creates a box called DAVIDSAGE, and stores the number 10 in it.

Type

    LET PAYFORDAVID=5*DAVIDSAGE

This command creates a box called PAYFORDAVID. The value assigned to PAYFORDAVID is calculated by multiplying 5 by the number in the DAVIDSAGE box. This number is 10. 5 times 10 makes 50, so the box called PAYFORDAVID should contain 50.

Type

    PRINT PAYFORDAVID
            50

and check that it contains 50.

50

PAYFORDAVID

Type

    PRINT DAVIDSAGE
            10

and check that it still contains 10. The value of a variable is not changed if it appears on the right-hand side of the = in an assignment command (for example LET ... = 5*DAVIDSAGE). The computer simply finds out what value is in the box called DAVIDSAGE, and then uses that value in its calculations.

- -

Type

    LET MARTINSAGE=9
    PRINT MARTINSAGE
            9

9

MARTINSAGE

Type

    LET MARTINSAGE=MARTINSAGE+1

Although this command may look rather odd at first, the computer processes it in a similar way to the last exercise. Firstly it gets the value held in MARTINSAGE, which is 9. Then it adds 1, giving 10. Finally it assigns the value 10 to MARTINSAGE.

Type

    PRINT MARTINSAGE
            10

10

MARTINSAGE

and check that it is correct. Note that the previous value (9) has been lost.

- -

The numbers in the boxes below show the values that will be
stored in the computer's memory after the following LET commands
have been executed.

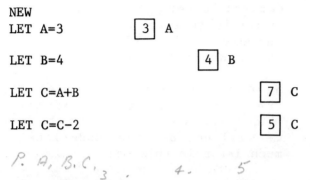

NEW
LET A=3   3 A

LET B=4   4 B

LET C=A+B   7 C

LET C=C-2   5 C

P. A, B, C,
        3   4.   5

Type these commands into the computer, and check (using PRINT
commands) that the values in the computer's memory boxes agree
with the values above.

- -

Again, the numbers in the boxes below show the values that will
be stored in the computer's memory after the following LET
commands have been executed. However, a deliberate mistake has
been made. Can you spot it?

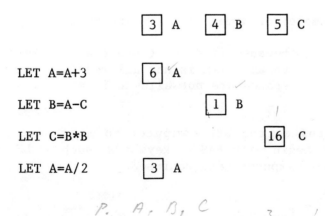

                3 A   4 B   5 C

LET A=A+3   6 A

LET B=A-C   1 B

LET C=B*B   16 C

LET A=A/2   3 A

            P. A, B, C   3.

Type these commands into the computer, and see (using PRINT
commands) whether the computer finds the same mistake as you did.

- -

2.2 Variable names

To finish this unit we look more closely at variable names.

The BASIC on the BBC computer allows names of any length. There are some rules, however.

1) It can contain   capital letters (A, B,... Z);
small letters (a, b,... z);
numbers (0, 1,... 9);
the 'underline' character.

No other characters may be used. Because there is a danger of confusing the 'underline' character with the 'minus', we will not use the 'underline' until much later in this book.

2) A name must start with a letter.

3) Spaces are not allowed in the middle of a name.

The following are examples of correct names:

```
GALLONS
AD1984
AGE
```

The following are examples of names that are incorrect:

```
55BC            because it doesn't start with a letter.
PETER*SMITH     an asterisk is not allowed in a name.
GOALS IN MONTH  spaces are not allowed in a name.
```

You have to be careful on the BBC computer to make sure that variable names do not begin with BASIC "keywords" such as LET and PRINT. If they do, the computer gets confused.

Type
```
LET LETTER=9
LET PRINTER=5
```

LETTER is invalid because it starts with the letters LET. PRINTER is wrong because it starts with the letters PRINT. You should avoid names beginning with:

```
COS     for example COST
END     for example ENDING
FOR     for example FORM
LEN     for example LENGTH
LET     for example LETTER
NEW     for example NEWVALUE
OLD     for example OLDVALUE
POS     for example POSITION
PRINT   for example PRINTER
REM     for example REMAINDER
TO      for example TOTAL
VAL     for example VALUE
```

One way round this problem is to use only small letters for variable names. This requires greater skill at typing, however, because you are continually using the SHIFT key. Until you become good at typing, you will find it easier to use capital letters for variable names, and avoid using names which begin with BASIC keywords. With a bit of practice this becomes straightforward.

Questions

1.   Name the BASIC commands which you have met in this book so far.   *LET.*

2.   What is the name of the part of a computer that stores information?   *MEMORY*

3.   What is a <u>variable</u> in BASIC?   *The ~~contents of~~ a named box its contents can be altered.*

4.   What is an <u>assignment</u> in BASIC?   *The LET command is called an assignment.*

5.   Write an assignment command which will assign the value 23 to a variable called DAY.   *LET DAY = 23*
P. DAY

6.   Which are the variables in the following assignment?

    LET CENTIGRADE=FAHRENHEIT*5/9

7.   What happens if you try to use a variable which has not yet been assigned a value?

8.   What is the purpose of the NEW command?

9.   Work out what values will be in the memory boxes after the computer has processed each of the following commands. Write your answers in the boxes provided.

	your answers	computer
LET A=8	[8] A	[ ] A
LET B=A/2	[4] B	[ ] B
LET C=A−B	[4] C	[ ] C
LET C=4−C	[0] C	[ ] C

Now type the commands into the computer, and check (using PRINT commands) that your answers are correct.

```
LET A = 8
P. A
     8
LET B = A/2
P. B
     4
LET C = A-B
P. A-B
     4
LET C = 4-C
P. 4-C
     0

P. A, B. C. C
```

3 What is a program?

Up to now, whenever you have typed a command at the keyboard the computer has executed it immediately. If you want the computer to do the same thing again you must re-enter the command. This can be boring. It would be nice if there was a way of saving commands somewhere, and then telling the computer to execute the commands you have saved. This unit describes how to do this.

A program is a sequence of commands. Each line of a program consists of a line-number followed by a command. For example:

```
1 LET AGE=10
2 PRINT AGE
3 LET PAY=5*AGE
4 PRINT PAY
5 END
```

The program is stored in the computer's memory. You can tell the computer to execute the commands of the program by typing RUN. In response, the computer will fetch from memory the command contained in Line 1 of the program, and execute it. Then the computer will fetch the command contained in Line 2, and execute that. This continues until it reaches the end of the program. As you can see, the line-numbers tell the computer the order in which the commands are to be executed.

In the example program shown above, we have used one command per line. BBC BASIC actually allows you to put several commands on one line, but we will deal with this later. At this stage, only use one command per line.

```
**************************************************************
*                                                          *
*     A program is a sequence of commands.                 *
*                                                          *
*     The RUN command tells the computer to execute the program *
*     stored in its memory. This is called running the program. *
*                                                          *
**************************************************************
```

How do we get a program into the computer's memory in the first place? Easy. Simply type the line-number, followed by the command, and repeat for each line of the program.

PRACTICAL EXERCISES

- -

Remembering the line-numbers, type

```
1 LET AGE=10
2 PRINT AGE
```

Notice that the computer simply accepts what you type, and then displays its prompt, waiting for another command. It does not execute the commands; if it did, you would see the number 10 appear on the screen, resulting from the PRINT AGE command.

Type

```
3 LET PAY=5*AGE
4 PRINT PAY
5 END
```
        RUN   10   50:

The program should now be in the computer's memory.

- -

Type
        LIST

The LIST command causes the program stored in memory to be displayed on the screen. Check each line and make sure that the program is correct. If any line is wrong, then just re-type that line (not forgetting the line-number).

- -

Type
        RUN

The numbers 10 and 50 should be displayed on the screen. The 10 results from Line 2 (PRINT AGE) being executed. The 50 results from Line 4 (PRINT PAY) being executed.

- -

Type
        TRACE ON
        RUN

The computer should display:

```
<1>  <2>            10
<3>  <4>            50
<5>
```

The TRACE command tells the computer to print out the line-number of a command before it executes that command. Hence, you can see which lines the computer has executed. The numbers between the < > pairs are the line-numbers. Line 1 is displayed first because it was executed first; then comes Line 2, followed by the display of 10 resulting from the PRINT AGE command; Line 3 is next; then Line 4, followed by the display of 50 resulting from the PRINT PAY command; finally Line 5 is executed. This very useful TRACE facility that the BBC computer provides isn't available on a lot of other computers.

Type

```
     TRACE OFF
```

This tells the computer to stop tracing. Try the RUN command again, and confirm that the computer is no longer printing line-numbers.

- -

Type

```
     NEW
     LIST
```

In Unit 2 we saw that the NEW command tells the computer to forget about all variable names. In addition, it tells the computer to forget about the program in its memory. In fact, the NEW command clears memory completely. Hence, the LIST command has no effect, because there is now no program in memory.

- -

Type

```
     5 END
     2 PRINT AGE
     1 LET AGE=10
     LIST
```

Even though we typed the program in reverse order, the computer stores the program in its memory in line-number order.

Type

```
3 LET PAY=5*AGE
4 PRINT PAY
LIST
```

Again, the computer maintains the program in line-number order. Line 3 is inserted after Line 2, and Line 4 is inserted after Line 3. Check that the program runs as before.

- -

In the last exercise we were able to insert two lines in the middle of the program, between Line 2 and Line 5, by giving them line-numbers of 3 and 4. We couldn't insert another line, however, because there aren't any more unused line-numbers. Instead of using line-numbers of 1, 2, 3,... etc., it is common to make the first line of a program line-number 10, the second line of the program line-number 20, and so on. In this way, there are nine unused line-numbers between any two lines, and so up to nine lines can be inserted, if necessary.

BBC BASIC provides the AUTO command to generate line-numbers automatically when you are typing in a program. This makes entering programs simpler, because you need type only the commands.

Type

```
NEW
AUTO
```

10 should appear on the screen. Type   LET AGE=10 <u>RETURN</u>
20 should appear on the screen. Type   PRINT AGE <u>RETURN</u>
30 should appear on the screen. Type   LET PAY=5*<u>AGE RETURN</u>
40 should appear on the screen. Type   PRINT PAY <u>RETURN</u>
50 should appear on the screen. Type   END <u>RETURN</u>
60 should appear on the screen. Press   <u>ESCAPE</u>

To terminate automatic line-numbering you must press the ESCAPE key.

Type

```
LIST
```

and check that your program is correct. If any line is incorrect, then simply re-type that line (not forgetting the line-number).

Handwritten (top):
```
REM DIST.
15 INPUT S
20 P, "SPEED IS   "; S; "M.P.h"
40. INPUT T
50. P. "TIME TAKEN IS "; T; "h rs"
60 LET D = S * T
65. P. "DISTANCE IS  "; D; "miles"
70 END.
```
INPUT (written to left of line 20)

Type

    TRACE ON
    RUN
    TRACE OFF

and check that the program works correctly. Notice that the computer executes the line with the smallest line-number (10) first, then the line with the next smallest line-number (20), and so on.

Handwritten:
```
RUN. ? 60
SPEED IS 60 MPh
? 4
TIME TAKEN IS 4 hrs
DIST IS 240 miles
```

Handwritten (right/middle):
```
50 LET DISTANCE = SPEED * TIME
60 P. DISTANCE
70 END
RUN
60, 240

NEW
AUTO
LIST
RUN
TRACE ON
  & OFF
```

Questions

1. Name the new commands that you have met in this unit.

2. What is a **program**? *A sequence of commands.*

3. How do you tell the computer to **run** a program? *By typing RUN*

4. Where is the program stored while it is being run? *MEMORY*

5. What happens to the program in the computer's memory when you type NEW? *IT IS LOST.*

6. What is the purpose of a line-number? *TO WRITE A PROGRAM.*

7. Why do you normally use line-numbers of 10, 20, 30... ? *SO THAT ADDITIONAL LINES CAN BE INSERTED.*

8. What is the purpose of the TRACE command? *IT TELLS THE COMPUTER TO PRINT OUT THE LINE-NUMBER OF A COMMAND BEFORE EXECUTION*

9. What command do you use to display a program on the screen? *LIST*

10. When you are typing a program into your computer, what command will cause the computer to generate line-numbers automatically? *AUTO*

11* The distance that a car travels in a certain time can be calculated by multiplying its speed by the time. Using variable names of SPEED, HOURS and MILES, write a program to calculate the distance travelled in 4 hours when travelling at 60 miles per hour. The program should display the speed, the time and the distance on the screen, in this order. Type the program into the computer, list it and check that you have typed it correctly. Now run the program, and check that it produces the correct answer.

4 Input and output

4.1 The PRINT command

```
10 LET AGE=10
20 PRINT AGE
30 LET PAY=5*AGE
40 PRINT PAY
50 END
```

When it is run, this pocket money program displays two numbers on the screen. These numbers are 10 and 50. From our knowledge of the program, we know that 10 means '10 years of age', and 50 means '50 pence per week'. However, someone not familiar with the program is unlikely to know this. This section describes how we can make output easier to understand.

So far we have used the PRINT command in two ways:

PRINT 2+3   : the computer works out 2 add 3, and then displays the answer on the screen.

PRINT AGE   : the computer displays on the screen the number stored in the memory box called AGE.

Type

```
PRINT "HELLO"
```

The computer displays HELLO on the screen. We can get the computer to display any message on the screen by using a PRINT command of this form. The message is written between two quotation marks ("...........").

What will be displayed by the command PRINT "AGE"?

Type

```
PRINT "AGE"
```

Were you correct? Now type

```
LET AGE=10
PRINT AGE
```

The command PRINT AGE tells the computer to display the contents
of the box called AGE (10 in this case). The command PRINT "AGE"
tells the computer to display the word AGE. It is important that
you understand clearly the difference between these two cases.
Using AUTO, type the following program into the computer:

```
10 PRINT "A"
20 PRINT "B";
30 PRINT "C"
40 PRINT "D"
50 END
```

Did you notice the semi-colon in Line 20? If not, retype the
line. Now run the program. You should see the following output:

```
A
BC
D
```

The cursor is the name given to the marker that the computer
displays on the screen to show you where the next character will
appear. Cursors vary from computer to computer – on the BBC
computer it is a flashing underline character.

PRINT "A"   tells the computer to display the letter A at the
                 cursor position, and then to move the cursor to
                 the beginning of the next line.
PRINT "B";   tells the computer to display the letter B at the
                 cursor position. The ; at the end of the command
                 tells the computer to leave the cursor on the same
                 line, immediately following the B. The cursor is
                 NOT moved to the beginning of the next line.
PRINT "C"   tells the computer to display the letter C at the
                 cursor position. Hence, the C is displayed
                 immediately after the B. The cursor is then moved
                 to the beginning of the next line.
PRINT "D"   is the same as for A and C.

```
***************************************************************
*                                                             *
*     If there is no semi-colon at the end of a PRINT command, *
*     the cursor is moved to the beginning of the next line.   *
*                                                             *
*     If there is a semi-colon at the end of a PRINT command,  *
*     the cursor is left on the same line as the output.       *
*                                                             *
***************************************************************
```

PRACTICAL EXERCISES

What output would you expect this program to produce?

```
10 PRINT "123";
20 PRINT "45"
30 PRINT "6";
40 PRINT "78"
50 END
```

123 45
6 78

Try it on your computer, and see if you were right.

Enter into the computer the pocket money program shown at the start of this unit (don't forget to type NEW before you start).

Type *10 LET AGE = 10*
```
     15 PRINT "AGE = ";
     35 PRINT "POCKET MONEY = ";
     LIST
```
20 PRINT AGE
*30 LET PAY = 5 * AGE*
40 PRINT PAY
50 (END)

You have inserted two extra lines into the program. Now run the program. The output should be:

```
AGE = 10
POCKET MONEY = 50
```

Is the output as you would expect? Notice that both Line 15 and Line 35 have a semi-colon at the end of the line.

Type
```
     15 PRINT "AGE = "
     35 PRINT "POCKET MONEY = "
     LIST
     RUN
```

Note the effect of missing off the semi-colons.

Up to now we have only used the PRINT command with one item, for example PRINT AGE. BASIC allows us to include a number of items in one PRINT command; the items are separated by semi-colons. When the command is executed by the computer, all the items will be displayed on one line.

Type

      PRINT "ABC" ; "123" ; "DE" ; "45"

You should see ABC123DE45 displayed on the screen. The spaces around the semi-colons are not necessary - they have been included simply to make the command easier to read.

- -

Type

      LET AGE=10
      PRINT "AGE = ";AGE

and you should see AGE = 10 displayed on the screen. Notice that there are two items in the PRINT command ("AGE = " and AGE).

- -

Our pocket money program now becomes:

      10 LET AGE=10
      20 PRINT "AGE = ";AGE
      30 LET PAY=5*AGE
      40 PRINT "POCKET MONEY = ";PAY
      50 END

Type this program into the computer, and see if it works correctly.

- -

4.2 The INPUT command

Our pocket money program works well for a boy or girl who is aged 10. Suppose, however, that we want to work out the pocket money for David, who is 12 years old. As it stands, the program will not work. We must change Line 10 to LET AGE=12, and then run the program.

Type

      10 LET AGE=12
      LIST
      RUN

and see if the results are correct.

      If we now want to work out the pocket money for Martin, who is 9 years old, we will have to change the program yet again. This is becoming very boring. This difficulty can be overcome by using the INPUT command.

Type

```
10 INPUT AGE
LIST
RUN
```

When the computer executes the INPUT AGE command, it displays a question mark on the screen, and waits for you to type a value on the keyboard. This value is then stored in the memory box called AGE.

Type

```
10          in response to the ?, and press the RETURN key.
```

The output should be the same as we obtained previously for a 10 year old.

Type

```
RUN
and   5          in response to the ?, and press the RETURN key.
```

Has the computer produced the correct answer? We can now run the program as often as we like, and obtain the pocket money for whatever age we enter.

```
*****************************************************************
*                                                               *
*    The INPUT X command accepts a number typed at the keyboard *
*    and stores this number in the memory box called X.         *
*                                                               *
*****************************************************************
```

When the computer executes the INPUT command in the pocket money program, and it displays the ? on the screen, we know that the computer is asking us to enter the child's age because we are familiar with the program. However, someone not familiar with the program is unlikely to know this. The problem is the same as we met when dealing with output (the numbers 10 and 50), and it can be overcome in exactly the same way.

Type

```
5 PRINT "ENTER AGE ";          10 INPUT AGE
LIST
RUN
```

When the computer executes Line 5, it will display the message ENTER AGE on the screen. The semi-colon at the end causes the cursor to remain on the same line. Line 10 displays the ?, and then we can type a number (say 10). The program then continues exactly as before.

The message can be included in the INPUT command itself. For example

```
10 INPUT "ENTER AGE ",AGE
```

has the same effect as the two lines

```
 5 PRINT "ENTER AGE";
10 INPUT AGE
```

Making this change, our pocket money program now becomes:

```
10 INPUT "ENTER AGE ",AGE
20 LET PAY=5*AGE
30 PRINT "POCKET MONEY = ";PAY
40 END
```

Notice that the PRINT "AGE = ";AGE command is no longer needed, because we can see the age from the message produced by Line 10.

ENTER AGE ? 10

POCKET MONEY = 50.

Questions

1. What new commands have you met in this unit? *INPUT*

2. What output will the following program produce?

```
10 PRINT "A"
20 PRINT "BB";
30 PRINT "CCC"
40 PRINT "DDDD"
50 END
```

A
BB CCC
DDDD

3. Type in the program, run it and see if you were correct.

4. What output will the following program produce?

```
10 PRINT "A";"B";
20 PRINT "C";"D"
30 PRINT "E";"F"
40 END
```

A B C
C D
E F
F.

5.   Type in the program, run it and see if you were correct.

6.   Write an INPUT command which has the same effect as:

PRINT "ENTER WEEKLY AMOUNT ";   *INPUT "ENTER WEEKLY AMOUNT ",WEEKLY*
INPUT WEEKLY

7.   How can you stop the cursor moving to the next line after a PRINT command is executed?

8*   In the present version of the pocket money program, the weekly amount for each year of the child's life is fixed at 5 pence per week. Modify the program so that this amount can be entered from the keyboard.

Hints:

  a) you will need another INPUT command between Line 10 and Line 20, asking for the weekly amount. Use a variable called WEEKLY.
  b) you will need to replace Line 20 by a line that calculates PAY by multiplying WEEKLY by AGE, rather than 5 by AGE.

Type the program into the computer, and then run it. When the program has run, the screen should look something like:

    ENTER AGE ?10
    ENTER WEEKLY AMOUNT ?6
    POCKET MONEY = 60

9*   Modify the program you produced for question 8 so that the words PENCE PER WEEK are added to the final line of output. An example line of output is:

    POCKET MONEY = 60 PENCE PER WEEK

Hint : you will need to modify Line 30.

5 Looking after your programs

5.1 Backing store

A program is a sequence of commands. When the computer is given the RUN command, it will execute the program stored in its memory. Type the following program into your computer.

```
10 PRINT "I AM A CLEVER COMPUTER"
20 PRINT "GOOD BYE"
30 END
```

Type
```
LIST
RUN
```

Does the program work correctly? Now switch off your computer, and then switch it back on again.

Type
```
LIST
```

You should find that the program has disappeared. If you want to run this program again, you will have to re-type it all.

```
*****************************************************************
*                                                               *
*    A computer's memory is cleared when the computer is        *
*    switched off, and any program it contains is lost.         *
*                                                               *
*****************************************************************
```

It is boring to have to type in a program every time you want to use it. Therefore, nearly all computers provide a memory in which programs can be saved even when the computer is switched off. This memory is called a backing store. Cassette tapes are the most common form of 'backing store' on small computers. Larger, and more expensive computers, may use 'floppy disks'. This book deals only with cassette tapes.

5.2 The SAVE command

Recording a program on tape is just like recording music on tape; you can play the cassette back later, and the music will still be there. You will need to give a name to each program that you save on tape. The number of characters that you can use in the name varies from computer to computer; on the BBC computer the maximum is 10 characters. The name you choose should be meaningful in the sense that it reminds you of the purpose of the program. For example:

"STARWARS"   for a 'starwars' program.

"POCKMONEY"   for our 'pocket money' program. Note that the name has been shortened because there are 11 letters in the words 'pocket money', which exceeds the maximum allowed (10).

People modify programs after they have been written, and often keep several versions of the same program. If you use 9 characters or less for the program name, then there will be a spare character which can be used for the version number. For example, "POCKMONEY1" for version 1 of the pocket money program, "POCKMONEY2" for version 2, and so on.

It is good practice to start every program with a program header to give a title to the program. With its header, the pocket money program becomes:

```
10 REM  POCKET MONEY PROGRAM  (POCKMONEY1)
20
30 INPUT "ENTER AGE ",AGE
40 LET PAY=5*AGE
50 PRINT "POCKET MONEY = ";PAY
60 END
```

Line 10   is the 'program header'. REM is short for REMARK. We use remarks in BASIC when we want to include some lines to make the purpose of the program clearer to us. When the computer executes a REM command, it ignores everything else on that line. Hence, a REMark is purely for the reader's benefit. The name in the brackets (POCKMONEY1) is the name under which this program is saved on cassette.

Line 20   is a blank line to separate the header from the rest of the program. This line is not essential, but it does make the program more readable. To insert a blank line into a program:

1.   press the space bar once;
2.   then press the RETURN key.

Pressing the RETURN key by itself will not produce a
blank line.

If you were to unwind a cassette tape, you would find it similar
to the following diagram:

leader	brown tape	leader

Most of the tape is brown, and it is on this part of the cassette
that programs are recorded. Both sides of the tape can be used,
simply by turning the cassette over. The length of the tape
depends on the capacity of the cassette. For example:

a C15 cassette provides 15 minutes recording (seven-and-a-
half minutes on each side);

a C60 cassette provides 60 minutes recording (30 minutes on
each side);

Fixed to either end of the brown tape there is a short plastic
'leader'. These leaders attach the tape to the two spools inside
the cassette.

IT IS IMPORTANT TO REMEMBER THAT PROGRAMS CANNOT BE
RECORDED ON THESE LEADERS.

PRACTICAL EXERCISES

- -
Many of the units in this book require you to save programs on a
cassette. One long cassette (C60) is probably better than three
or four shorter ones (C15's) so far as this book is concerned.
Acquire two C60 cassettes (one for backup - see Section 5.5).

- -
Every cassette should be given a name which reflects the purpose
of the programs on that cassette. A suitable name for our
cassette might be UNIT PROGRAMS, reflecting the fact that the
programs on it are the programs associated with the units of this
book. If your cassette has a label already, then write UNIT

PROGRAMS on this label. If not, then get a sticky label, write UNIT PROGRAMS on it, and stick the label to the cassette.

- -

Insert the cassette into your recorder, with Side 1 uppermost. Rewind the tape, and set the tape counter to 000 (if your recorder has one).

- -

Take the cassette out of the recorder. The 'leader' should now be visible. Wind the tape forwards by hand until all this leader has moved onto the right-hand spool, and you can see the brown tape. Put the cassette back into the recorder. It is now ready for recording programs.

- -

You cannot see the programs recorded on a cassette. However, you can use a <u>cassette contents sheet</u> to help you to remember the programs that are stored on the cassette. Every time you save a program on the cassette, add its name, and the final tape counter reading, to the Contents Sheet.

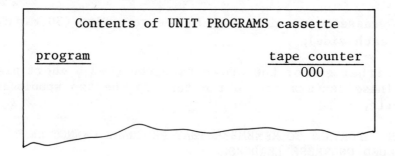

Make a 'cassette contents' sheet for your UNIT PROGRAMS cassette, as shown above. This sheet should be kept with the cassette.

- -

Type the pocket money program into the computer. List it, and then run it to make sure that it is working correctly.

- -

The SAVE command saves on cassette the program in your computer's memory.

1.   Type   SAVE "POCKMONEY1"

      The message 'RECORD then RETURN' will be displayed on the screen.

2.   Press the RECORD button on your recorder. The tape should
      start moving.

3.   Pause for 2-3 seconds, to produce a short gap on the tape.

4.   Press the RETURN key on the keyboard.

      The computer will record the program on the tape. When the
      computer has finished, the > prompt will appear on the
      screen. If your cassette has automatic motor control, then
      the tape will stop automatically. If it hasn't, you will
      have to stop the recorder manually.

5.   Release the RECORD button on your recorder.

- -

Add the name of the program (POCKMONEY1), and the final reading
of the tape counter, to the 'cassette contents' sheet, as shown
below:

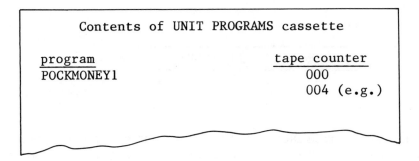

Contents of UNIT PROGRAMS cassette

program	tape counter
POCKMONEY1	000
	004 (e.g.)

000   is the position of the start of POCKMONEY1
004   is the position of the end of POCKMONEY1. It also becomes
      the position of the start of the next program that you save
      on the cassette.

- -

Type the following program into your computer:

```
NEW
10 REM  A DEMONSTRATION PROGRAM  (CLEVER1)
20
30 PRINT "I AM A CLEVER COMPUTER"
40 PRINT "GOOD BYE"
50 END
```

Make sure that the program is working correctly.

- -

Now save this program on the tape immediately after POCKMONEY1, calling it CLEVER1. The steps are similar to those you used to save POCKMONEY1, except that the SAVE command is SAVE "CLEVER1".

- -

Add the name of the program (CLEVER1), and the final reading of the tape counter, to the 'cassette contents' sheet, as shown below:

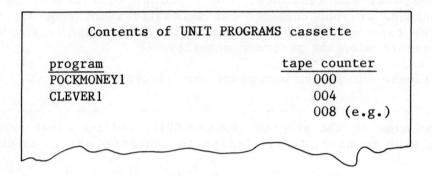

Contents of UNIT PROGRAMS cassette	
program	tape counter
POCKMONEY1	000
CLEVER1	004
	008 (e.g.)

The layout of the tape is now:

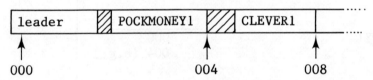

| leader | | POCKMONEY1 | | CLEVER1 | |
000   004   008

The shaded areas represent short gaps between the programs. These gaps are caused by the pause between pressing the RECORD button, and pressing the RETURN key, when saving programs.

- -

5.3 The LOAD command

The LOAD command loads a program into the computer's memory from cassette.

- -

1.   Insert the UNIT PROGRAMS cassette into the recorder.

2.   Type

        LOAD "POCKMONEY1"

     The message SEARCHING will be displayed.

3.   Rewind the tape.

4.   Start the cassette playing by pressing the PLAY button on
      the recorder. Whenever the computer finds a program on the
      tape, it will display its name on the screen. If that
      program happens to be the one it is looking for, it will
      also display the message LOADING. When the loading is
      complete, the > prompt will reappear. If your cassette has
      automatic motor control, the tape will stop automatically;
      otherwise, you will have to stop the recorder manually.

5.   Release the PLAY button on your cassette.

- -
The program is now in the computer's memory. List it, and check
that it is correct. Now run the program. Does it perform
correctly?

- -
With the UNIT PROGRAMS cassette as it was at the end of the last
exercise, type

      LOAD ""

and press the PLAY button on your recorder. The two quotes are
typed one after the other with no space between. If you omit the
program name in the LOAD command, and just type LOAD "", then the
computer will load the next program on the tape, no matter what
it is called. In this case, CLEVER1 should be loaded.

- -
List the program, and check that it is correct. Now run the
program. Does it perform correctly?

- -

5.4 Cataloguing a cassette

The simplest way to find out what programs are saved on any
cassette is to rewind the cassette to the beginning, and then
issue a LOAD command for a program that you know isn't on the
tape (e.g. LOAD "ABCDEF"). The computer will scan the entire tape
looking for this program. As it does so, however, it will display
the name of each program that it encounters on the tape.
      Some computers provide a special command for displaying a
catalogue on the screen. In the case of the BBC computer, this
command is *CAT.

PRACTICAL EXERCISES

- -

Rewind the cassette to the beginning. Tell the computer to load a program called ABCDEF. As this program isn't on the tape, the computer will search the whole tape, and it will display a catalogue of the cassette. The programs should be POCKMONEY1 and CLEVER1.

- -

Repeat the previous exercise using the *CAT command.

- -

5.5 Backup

A cassette occasionally develops a fault which prevents one of its programs from being loaded into memory. When this occurs, the program is lost. Sometimes, several programs from one cassette may be lost. The solution to this problem is to keep a duplicate copy on a separate cassette. If your cassette becomes corrupted, you should still be able to retrieve the program from the duplicate cassette. This process is called backup, and the duplicate cassette is called the backup cassette. Each of your cassettes should have its own backup cassette. These should be kept in a safe place separate from the main cassettes, so that any mishap occurring to the main ones is unlikely to affect the backup cassettes as well.

PRACTICAL EXERCISES

- -

Rewind the UNIT PROGRAMS cassette.

Type

    LOAD ""

The computer should load POCKMONEY1. When it is loaded, list it and then run it. Does it perform correctly? Take the cassette out of the recorder. Do not rewind the tape.

- -

Select your other C60 cassette to be your backup cassette, and then write UNIT PROGRAMS BACKUP on its label. Put the cassette into the recorder, and save the program in the computer's memory at position 000 on the tape, calling it POCKMONEY1 (don't forget the leader). Take the cassette out of the recorder. Do not rewind the tape.

- -

Load CLEVER1 from your UNIT PROGRAMS cassette, and save it as CLEVER1 on your backup cassette, immediately after POCKMONEY1.

- -

Now produce a catalogue of the backup cassette to ensure that the copying has been carried out correctly. If all is satisfactory, then store the backup in a safe place.

- -

5.6 The OLD command

The NEW command clears the computer's memory in readiness for you typing in your next program. What happens if you accidently type NEW before you have saved your present program? With many computers, the program will be lost, and you will have to retype it all. The BBC computer provide a safety net. If you type OLD before you have entered any lines of the new program, then the previous program will be restored to memory.

PRACTICAL EXERCISES

- -

Load the POCKMONEY1 program from your cassette. List it and run it. Does it perform correctly?

Type

        NEW
        LIST

The program should have disappeared.

Type

        OLD
        LIST

The program should have been restored to memory.

Type

```
NEW
10 PRINT "NEW PROGRAM"
OLD
LIST
```

The 'old' program has really been lost, because a line of the 'new' program has been entered into memory.

- -

Questions

1.   What new commands have you met in this unit?

2.   What happens to the program in the computer's memory when the computer is switched off?

3.   What is a backing store?

4.   What is the purpose of the program header?

5.   What is the purpose of the SAVE command?

6.   If a program is stored on cassette as STARWARS3, what does the 3 mean?

7.   Why should you keep a cassette contents sheet?

8.   What will happen to your program if you try to record it on the plastic 'leader' at the start of a cassette?

9.   What is the purpose of the LOAD command?

10.   What is the effect of the command LOAD ""?

11.   How can you obtain a catalogue of the programs on a cassette?

12.   What is backup? Why is it necessary to backup your cassettes?

13.   What is the effect of the OLD command?

6 Editing

As we have already seen, programs are almost always altered after they have been written. The process of altering a program is called editing. This unit describes how you can edit BASIC programs.

6.1 Modifying whole lines

- -

Load the POCKMONEY1 program from your cassette. List it and run, and make sure that it is working correctly. Suppose we now want to make the computer appear a little more polite.

Type

```
30 INPUT "PLEASE ENTER YOUR AGE ",AGE
```

List and run the program. The previous Line 30 has been replaced by the line you have just typed in. ANY line can be replaced by typing a new line with the same line-number.

- -

Type

```
55 PRINT
56 PRINT "GOOD BYE"
57 PRINT
```

List and run the program. A new line can be inserted into a program by choosing its line-number to be BETWEEN the line-numbers of the lines above and below the new line. Hence, Lines 55, 56 and 57 are inserted between Line 50 and Line 60. Notice that a PRINT command by itself (as in Line 55) simply produces a blank line on the screen when it is executed by the computer.

- -

Type

```
RENUMBER
```

List and run the program. The program should run exactly as before. Note, however, that the line-numbers have been altered so that each line-number is 10 more than the previous one. You should always renumber the line-numbers after inserting lines, because programs whose line-numbers increase in regular steps are easier to understand.

- -

Type
```
RENUMBER 1,1
LIST
RENUMBER 100,100
LIST
RENUMBER 100,10
LIST
```

Look at each listing carefully. You should be able to work out that the RENUMBER n,m command alters the line-numbers so that the first line-number is n, and each subsequent line-number is m more than the previous one.

- -

Type
```
110 RETURN
LIST
```

Notice that Line 110 has been deleted. The simplest way to delete a single line is to type its line-number, and then press the RETURN key. Contrast this with inserting a blank line, where we type the line-number, a SPACE, and then press the RETURN key.

- -

Type
```
DELETE 150,170
LIST
```

A group of lines may be deleted by the DELETE command. Line 150, Line 170, and all the lines between 150 and 170 (in this example, only Line 160) are deleted.

- -

RENUMBER the program. It should now be:

```
10 REM   POCKET MONEY PROGRAM    (POCKMONEY1)
20 INPUT "PLEASE ENTER YOUR AGE ",AGE
30 LET PAY=5*AGE
40 PRINT "POCKET MONEY = ";PAY
50 END
```

```
***************************************************************
*                                                             *
* To replace a line:   type the new line with the same line-  *
*                       number as the line to be replaced.    *
*                                                             *
* To insert a line:    type the new line with a line-number   *
*                       BETWEEN the line-numbers of the lines  *
*                       above and below the new line.          *
*                                                             *
* To delete a line:    type the line-number by itself. To     *
*                       delete a group of lines, use DELETE x,y *
*                       where x is the smallest line-number of  *
*                       the group, and y is the largest.       *
*                                                             *
***************************************************************
```

6.2 Modifying part of a line

When you find an error in a line of your program, you can correct
it by retyping the whole line. The new line will replace the
previous line if it is given the same line-number. The BBC
computer provides a means by which you can correct PART of a line
without having to retype the WHOLE line.

screen

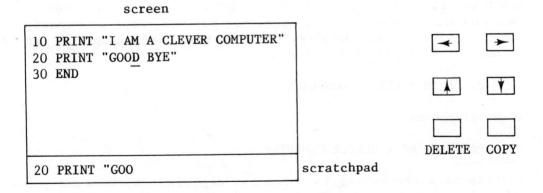

On the right-hand side of the keyboard of the BBC computer are
six special keys. The keys with the arrows on them allow you to
move the cursor to any point on the screen. As soon as you press
one of these arrow keys, the computer enters 'edit mode', and a
scratchpad appears on the screen. You construct your new line in
the scratchpad. Any characters typed at the keyboard are

displayed in the scratchpad. In addition, you can move the cursor to any line on the screen, and copy characters from that line into the scratchpad by pressing the COPY key. The underline of the D in Line 20 indicates the cursor. Characters are deleted from the scratchpad in the normal way using the DELETE key. Pressing the RETURN key takes the computer out of 'edit mode', and the line in the scratchpad becomes the new program line.

PRACTICAL EXERCISE

Use 'edit mode' on your computer to change the following lines of the pocket money program:

        20 INPUT "PLEASE TYPE YOUR AGE ",AGE
        40 PRINT "YOUR POCKET MONEY IS ";PAY;" PENCE PER WEEK"

List and run the program.

6.3 Abbreviations

A lot of typing is often needed to enter a program into the computer, and if you haven't had a lot of practice, it can take quite a long time. Therefore computers often provide facilities to reduce the amount of typing you have to do.

Expanded abbreviations.   The BBC computer allows BASIC words to be abbreviated when you type them in, but the computer expands the abbreviation, and displays the full word. For example P. can be used in place of PRINT. Hence,

      P. "I AM A CLEVER COMPUTER"

is displayed as

      PRINT "I AM A CLEVER COMPUTER"

In this case the saving is three key depressions, because you just type P and . instead of P, R, I, N, and T.
        Common abbreviations are:

        DEL. :   DELETE
        L.   :   LIST
        P.   :   PRINT
        REN. :   RENUMBER

Omissions.   BASIC keywords can sometimes be missed out. For
example, most versions of BASIC allow the keyword LET to be left
out of an assignment command. Hence

       20 LET PAY=5*AGE

can be written as

       20 PAY=5*AGE

Most programs written in BASIC leave out the LET, and you are
advised to do the same. All the programs in this book after this
point will leave out the LET in assignment commands.

Questions

1.   What is meant by editing?

2.   How do you replace a line in a program?

3.   How do you insert a new line into a program?

4.   How do you delete a line from a program?

5.   How do you delete a group of lines from a program?

6.   What is the effect of the RENUMBER command?

7 REPEAT loops

A program is a sequence of commands. In all the programs we have met so far, the computer executes the first command, then it executes each of the following commands in turn, until it reaches the END of the program. If we want to use the pocket money program to find the pocket money of several children, then we have to RUN the program several times, and enter a different age on each run. What we would like to be able to do is to run the program ONCE, and during that run get the computer to execute a group of commands over and over again, until we tell it to stop. This can be written as:

```
repeat
     a group of commands
until told to stop
```

This can be translated into BASIC very easily on the BBC computer. The pocket money program becomes:

```
10 REPEAT
20   INPUT "ENTER AGE ",AGE
30   PAY=5*AGE
40   PRINT "POCKET MONEY = ";PAY
50 UNTIL told to stop
60 END
```

The REPEAT command in Line 10 tells the computer to execute over and over again all the commands between Line 10 and the UNTIL in Line 50. Hence, Lines 20, 30 and 40 form the group of commands to be repeated. How can we tell the computer to finish its repetition? As we are not interested in the pocket money of a child whose age is zero, we could use a zero value of age to tell the computer to finish repeating the group of commands. Hence, Line 50 becomes:

```
50 UNTIL AGE=0
```

Notice that we have typed two spaces at the start of Lines 20, 30 and 40. This is known as <u>indentation</u>. We indent the group of commands between the REPEAT and the UNTIL so as to make the program easier to read. If there are several REPEAT commands in a program, and you are not using indentation, then it isn't always easy to see which UNTIL belongs to a particular REPEAT. With indentation it is obvious.

PRACTICAL EXERCISES

- -
Type

```
10 REPEAT
20    INPUT "ENTER AGE ",AGE
30    PAY=5*AGE
40    PRINT "POCKET MONEY = ";PAY
50 UNTIL AGE=0
60 END
```

List and run the program. Try it with values of 5, 12, 7 and 0. You should be asked to ENTER AGE <u>four</u> times, and then the program should stop running. Does it work correctly?

- -
Type

```
45 ..PRINT   (replacing the two dots by two spaces).
```

List and run the program. Try it again with values of 5, 12, 7 and 0. It should produce the same results as before, but they should be displayed more clearly on the screen because of the blank line between each set of results (produced by the computer executing Line 45). You should always try to make your results as clear as possible.

- -
Type

```
TRACE ON
RUN
```

The computer should display:

<10> <20> ENTER AGE ?

The computer executes Line 10, and then waits at Line 20 for you to enter an age.

Type

```
5 RETURN
```

The computer stores this value in the memory box called AGE.

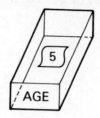

The computer should now display:

```
<30>  <40>   POCKET MONEY = 25
<45>
<50>  <20>   ENTER AGE ?
```

The computer executes Line 30, followed by Line 40, which causes POCKET MONEY = 25 to be displayed on the screen. Then it executes Line 45, producing a blank line on the screen.

Now the computer comes to Line 50 (UNTIL AGE=0). The computer gets the value contained in the memory box called AGE (5 in this example) and says 'is this equal to 0?'. Obviously it is not, so the computer goes back to the first line of the group of commands (Line 20) and asks you to enter the age again.

Type

        0 RETURN

The computer stores this value of 0 in the memory box called AGE. It now continues as it did above, displaying:

```
<30>  <40>   POCKET MONEY = 0
<45>
<50>  <60>
```

When the computer comes to Line 50, it gets the value contained in the AGE memory box (0 this time) and says 'is this equal to 0?'. It is. The computer has repeated the commands UNTIL AGE=0, and it is now time to stop the repetition. So the computer goes on to Line 60, which ends the program.

```
First  time through: it executes Lines    10 20 30 40 45 50
Second time through: it executes Lines       20 30 40 45 50
Other times through: it executes Lines       20 30 40 45 50
```

                    until it is told to stop.

The computer keeps returning to Line 20 and executing all the commands through to Line 50. This sort of structure is called a loop. The name 'loop' is used because the idea is similar to a loop in a piece of string – the string crosses itself just as the program appears to cross itself when the computer repeatedly executes the same commands (e.g. Lines 20-50). The group of commands being executed again and again is called the body of the loop. The commands controlling the number of times a loop is executed are known as loop control commands. Hence, a loop can be thought of as:

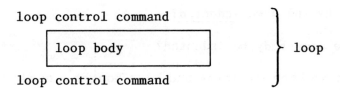

Notice that the loop 'body' is indented a few spaces so as to make it stand out. All loops have this general form. The loops described in this unit are called 'REPEAT loops' because they are controlled by the REPEAT command. In the next unit you will study a loop controlled by a different pair of loop control commands.

- -

Modify the pocket money program to become:

```
10 REM  POCKET MONEY PROGRAM  (POCKMONEY2)
20
30 REPEAT
40    INPUT "ENTER AGE ",AGE
50    PAY=5*AGE
60    PRINT "POCKET MONEY = ";PAY
70    PRINT
80 UNTIL AGE=0
90 END
```

List and run the program. Make sure that it is working correctly. It's a bit untidy printing the pocket money when AGE is 0; we will see in Unit 10 how to avoid this. Now save the program on your UNIT PROGRAMS cassette as POCKMONEY2. Don't forget to fill in the 'cassette contents' sheet.

- -

Questions

1.   What new commands have you met in this unit?

2.   What is a loop?

3.   Why is it called a 'loop'?

4.   What is the body of a loop?

5.   What are loop control commands?

6.   What is meant by the word indented?

7.   Why should the loop body be indented?

8*   Suppose you have been shopping and have bought a number of items. The shop gives you a bill showing you how much you paid for each item, and how much you paid altogether. Write a program to check that the bill is correct. Written in ordinary English, the program should be something like:

```
set bill to 0
repeat
  input item
    add item to bill
until item=0
print bill
end
```

Translate this into a BASIC program, and use variable names ITEM and BILL. List the program to check that it is correct, and then run it with the following data:

    the first item cost   5 pence;
    the second item cost 15 pence;
    the third item cost 11 pence.

Did you remember a value of 0 to finish the list? Does it work correctly? If not, go back and check.

8 FOR loops

8.1 The FOR command

In the last unit we saw how REPEAT loops are constructed in BASIC. REPEAT loops are usually used when you need repeatedly to execute a group of commands until some condition is satisfied. For example, you can enter as many ages into the pocket money program as you like – it makes no difference whether it is one age, or ten ages, or fifty-seven ages. The computer keeps on executing the group of commands within the loop until you enter an age of zero, at which point the program finishes.

There are many instances when you want to execute a group of commands a <u>fixed number of times</u>. FOR loops are used in this situation. The structure of a FOR loop is similar to the structure of a REPEAT loop.

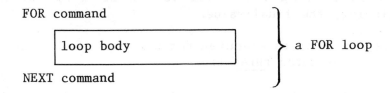

The FOR command marks the start of a FOR loop.

The NEXT command marks the end of a FOR loop.

The commands between the FOR command and the NEXT command make up the <u>body</u> of the loop. Notice that the loop body is indented just as it is in a REPEAT loop.

PRACTICAL EXERCISES

- -

Type
```
10 FOR K=1 TO 3
20    PRINT "K = ";K
30 NEXT K
40 END
```

List and run the program. The output should be:

    K = 1
    K = 2
    K = 3

The word FOR in the FOR command is followed by a variable name (we have used K in the example above). This variable is called the <u>loop-control-variable</u>. We can choose any variable to be the loop-control-variable, and we can specify a <u>start-value</u> and a <u>finish-value</u> by writing:

    FOR loop-control-variable = start-value TO finish-value

In our example above, we have used a start-value of 1, and a finish-value of 3. When the computer executes the FOR loop:

1.   it sets the loop-control-variable (K) to the start-value (1), and then it executes the commands in the body of the loop;
2.   it increases the value of the loop-control-variable by 1, and then it executes the commands in the loop body again;
3.   it repeats step 2 for all values of K up to, and including, the final-value.

In our example, the loop is executed for K values of 1, 2, and 3. Hence, the loop is executed <u>three</u> times.

- -

Modify your program to become:

    10 FOR K=3 TO 7
    20   PRINT "K = ";K   *loop control*
    30 NEXT K
    40 END

and run the program. The start-value can be any value: it does not have to be 1. In this example, the loop will be executed <u>five</u> times, with K values of 3, 4, 5, 6, and 7.

- -

Modify your program to become:

    10 FOR K=3 TO 7
    20   PRINT "HELLO"   *loop control*
    30 NEXT K
    40 END

and run the program. In the two examples before this one, we used the loop-control-variable as a variable within the body of the loop (we printed the value of K in Line 20). The loop-control-variable does not have to be used in the loop body. In the program above, we simply print HELLO five times, and the loop-control-variable serves merely to count the number of times that the loop is executed.

- -

Modify your program to become:

```
10 FOR K=3 TO 7
20    PRINT "K = ";K
40 END
```

EX ONLY ONCE
NEXT LEFT ON?

and run the program. The NEXT command marks the end of a loop. It tells the computer to go back to the start of the loop, and execute the loop again with the next value of the loop-control-variable, unless the final-value has already been reached.

If you omit the NEXT command, as we have done here, then the loop-control-variable will still be set to 3 by the FOR command, and the loop body will still be executed. However, as there is no NEXT command to send the computer back to Line 10, the program will finish at Line 40, and the loop will have been executed only once.

- -

Type

```
NEW
20    PRINT "HELLO"
30 NEXT K
40 END
```

MISTAKE

and run the program. Here, we have missed out the FOR command. As there is no FOR command to match the NEXT command at Line 30, the computer doesn't know which line to go to, and so it tells you that you have made a mistake.

```
*********************************************************************
*                                                                 *
*     FOR and NEXT commands are always used in pairs.             *
*                                                                 *
*********************************************************************
```

- -

Type

```
10 KSTART=3
20 FOR K=KSTART TO 7
30   PRINT "K = ";K
40 NEXT K
50 END
```

and run the program. A variable can be used to give the start-value; we have used KSTART here.

- -

Modify your program to become:

```
10 KSTART=3
15 KFINISH=7
20 FOR K=KSTART TO KFINISH
30   PRINT "K = ";K
40 NEXT K
50 END
```

and run the program. A variable can also be used to give the finish-value; we have used KFINISH here.

- -

Type
```
40 NEXT
```

and run the program. There does not <u>have</u> to be a variable after the NEXT in the NEXT command. However, it is good practice to write the name of the loop-control-variable there, because in larger programs with several FOR loops, it makes it easier to see which FOR this NEXT command belongs to.

- -

Type
```
40 NEXT KSTART
```

and run the program. The computer will display the error

    Can't Match FOR at Line 40.

There is no loop with KSTART as its loop-control-variable, and so the computer cannot find the FOR command to match this NEXT command.

- -

Modify your program to become:

```
10 FOR K=5 TO 3
20    PRINT "K = ";K
30 NEXT K
40 END
```

and run the program. The loop will be executed once, with K set to 5. Even though the start-value is greater than the final-value when the computer first encounters the FOR command, the loop will still be executed. It is only when the computer gets to the NEXT command that it compares the K value with the final-value, and is able to terminate the loop.

```
***************************************************************
*                                                             *
*    A FOR loop is ALWAYS executed at least once.             *
*                                                             *
***************************************************************
```

- -
Suppose you want the computer to work out and display 'tables'. The output for the 7-times table might be:

```
 1 TIMES 7 = 7
 2 TIMES 7 = 14
 3 TIMES 7 = 21
      ....
10 TIMES 7 = 70
```

You want to be able to select which particular table is displayed (7-times, 3-times, and so on), but for any table you want ten lines of output.

Type

```
10 REM  TABLES PROGRAM  (TABLES1)
20
30 INPUT "WHICH TABLE ",TABLE   7
40 FOR K=1 TO 10
50    ANSWER=K*TABLE       / X7
60    PRINT K;" TIMES ";TABLE;" = ";ANSWER
70 NEXT K
80 END
```

(handwritten annotation: / TIMES 7 = 7)

List the program, and check that you have typed it correctly. Now run the program.

Type

     7   when invited to enter a table.

The output should be:

```
1 TIMES 7 = 7
2 TIMES 7 = 14
3 TIMES 7 = 21
   ....
10 TIMES 7 = 70
```

The loop is executed ten times, because it is controlled by the command FOR K=1 TO 10, and K takes values of 1, 2,.. 10. A line of output is displayed on the screen each time Line 60 is executed, and so there are ten lines of output.

- -

When the program is working correctly, save it on your UNIT PROGRAMS cassette as TABLES1. Don't forget to fill in the 'cassette contents' sheet.

- -

8.2 Using a STEP in the FOR command

In all the examples we have used so far, the computer increases the value of the loop-control-variable by 1 each time it goes round the loop. We can extend the FOR command to include a STEP-value, so that each time the computer goes round the loop, it increases the loop-control-variable by this step-value.

- -

Type

```
10 FOR K=1 TO 5
20    PRINT "K = ";K
30 NEXT K
40 END
```

and run the program. The loop will be executed with K values of 1, 2, 3, 4, and 5.

- -

Modify Line 10 to become:

```
10 FOR K=1 TO 5 STEP 2
```

and run the program. The loop will now be executed with K values of 1, 3, and 5. In other words, the loop-control-variable increases in steps of 2.

- -

Modify Line 10 to become:

        10 FOR K=2 TO 9 STEP 3

and run the program. The loop will now be executed with K values of 2, 5, and 8.

- -

Modify Line 10 to become:

        10 FOR K=1 TO 5 STEP 1

and run the program. The loop will now be executed with K values of 1, 2, 3, 4, and 5. This is exactly the same as a FOR command of FOR K=1 TO 5. Hence, if you omit STEP from the FOR command, a step of 1 is assumed. Therefore

        FOR K=1 TO 5

is the same as

        FOR K=1 TO 5 STEP 1

- -

Modify Line 10 to become:

        10 FOR K=5 TO 1 STEP -2

and run the program. Notice that minus values can be used. In this example, the loop will be executed three times, with K values of 5, 3, and 1.

- -

Modify your program to become:

        10 FOR K=1 TO 5 STEP 2
        20   PRINT "K = ";K
        30 NEXT K
        40 PRINT "FINAL K = ";K
        50 END

and run the program. When the loop finishes, K has a value which is GREATER THAN the final-value.

Modify Line 10 to become:

     10 FOR K=5 TO 1 STEP −1

and run the program. In this case, K has a value of 0 when the
loop terminates. When the step is minus (−1 in this example), the
loop terminates when the loop-control-variable is LESS THAN the
final-value.

– –

Modify Line 10 to become:

     10 FOR K=1 TO 5 STEP 0

and run the program. Since we have specified a step of 0, the K
value will always be 1, and the loop will be executed for ever.
Press the ESCAPE key to terminate the program. You must avoid
using a step of 0.

– –

Questions

1.   What new commands have you met in this unit?

2.   What output will the following program produce?

     10 NUMBER=3
     20 FOR K=1 TO NUMBER
     30   PRINT K
     40 NEXT K
     50 END

Type in the program and then run it. Is the output as you expect?

3.   What output will the following program produce?

     10 KSTART=5
     20 KFINISH=9
     30 FOR K=KSTART TO KFINISH
     40   PRINT K
     50 NEXT K
     60 END

Type in the program and then run it. Is the output as you expect?

4.   What is the purpose of the STEP in the FOR command?

5.   What value of 'step' is used if you omit the STEP from the FOR command?

6.   What output will the following program produce?

```
10 FOR K=1 TO 30 STEP 10
20    PRINT K
30 NEXT K
40 END
```

Type in the program and then run it. Is the output as you expect?

7.   For each of the FOR commands below, write down in the boxes the value that K holds each time the loop is executed. Also fill in the value that K holds when the loop has terminated. The first has been done for you, to show you what to do:

FOR K=2 TO 3   the 1st time round the loop, K has a value of 2;
                  the 2nd time round the loop, K has a value of 3;
                  the loop now terminates, and K has a value of 4.

	value of K this time round the loop					value of K when loop terminated
	1st	2nd	3rd	4th	5th	
FOR K=2 TO 3	2	3	☐	☐	☐	4
FOR K=1 TO 5	☐	☐	☐	☐	☐	☐
FOR K=3 TO 6	☐	☐	☐	☐	☐	☐
FOR K=4 TO 7 STEP 2	☐	☐	☐	☐	☐	☐
FOR K=3 TO 7 STEP 5	☐	☐	☐	☐	☐	☐
FOR K=8 TO 5	☐	☐	☐	☐	☐	☐
FOR K=8 TO 5 STEP −1	☐	☐	☐	☐	☐	☐
FOR K=8 TO 5 STEP −3	☐	☐	☐	☐	☐	☐
FOR K=3 TO 6 STEP 0	☐	☐	☐	☐	☐	☐
FOR K=3 TO 6 STEP 1	☐	☐	☐	☐	☐	☐

Check your answers on the computer.

8.   Here is an alternative solution to the 'shopping' program described in Question 8 of Unit 7. Rewrite the program using proper indentation.

```
10 BILL=0
20 INPUT "ENTER NUMBER OF ITEMS ",NUMBER
30 PRINT
40 FOR K=1 TO NUMBER
50 PRINT "COST OF ITEM ";K;" = ";
60 INPUT ITEM
70 BILL=BILL+ITEM
80 NEXT K
90 PRINT
100 PRINT "TOTAL BILL = ";BILL
110 END
```

9.   Type your indented version into the computer, and run it with the following data:

5 <u>RETURN</u>

7 <u>RETURN</u>
3 <u>RETURN</u>
2 <u>RETURN</u>
4 <u>RETURN</u>
1 <u>RETURN</u>

10* Several errors can arise with FOR loops. How many different kinds of error can you think of? Four are mentioned in this Unit.

9 Random numbers

Many games are based on chance (sometimes called luck). This 'chance' is often provided by throwing a dice. For example, the game of 'Snakes and Ladders' involves the players moving counters on a board according to the number of spots shown on the face of a dice. These games often require you to throw a 'six' before you can start. Sometimes you can throw a 'six' almost immediately, yet at other times your luck seems to be out, and you have to wait a long time for a 'six'. Many games available on computers also involve 'chance'. For example, the computer may produce enemy space ships for you to shoot down, and these space ships seem to appear at random, with no apparent pattern. In contrast, all the programs we have written so far produce the same answers on every run of the program, so long as we provide the same data. This unit describes how we can tell the computer to produce what appears to be random behaviour.

PRACTICAL EXERCISES

- -

We can produce a random sequence of numbers in a BASIC program by using the RND command.

Type

```
10 FOR K=1 TO 10
20     X=RND(6)
30     PRINT X
40 NEXT K
50 END
```

List the program, and check that you have typed it correctly. Now run the program. Although your output will not be EXACTLY the same as the following, it should be similar:

```
2
1
5
6
4
1
2
3
4
4
```

These numbers look like the numbers you might get by throwing a
dice ten times. Line 20 generates a number at random, and stores
it in memory box X. The '6' in Line 20 tells the computer that
the number must be in the range 1-6 (that is, 1 or 2 or 3 or 4 or
5 or 6). To generate random numbers between 1 and 10, replace
RND(6) by RND(10).

- -

Now run the program again. You should obtain a different sequence
of ten numbers. Each time you run the program, the sequence
should be different, and you should not be able to PREDICT what
numbers will be displayed. In this sense, the numbers are said to
be random numbers.

- -

Questions

1.   What are random numbers?

2*   Write a program to make the computer look as if it is
tossing a coin twenty times. Hint: you could let 1 mean 'heads'
and 2 mean 'tails', and simply display 1's and 2's.

10 The IF command

10.1 The IF command

Decisions are part of everyday life. For example:

    IF you are hungry THEN eat some food.

    IF it is raining THEN put on a coat before going outside.

    IF you are tired THEN go to bed.

These examples all have the same form:

    IF some condition is true THEN take some action.

Taking the first example, the condition is 'you are hungry', and the action is 'eat some food'. If the condition is true, then you take the action.

A computer can also take decisions. Indeed, it is this capability which makes it into such a powerful and versatile piece of equipment. A computer can take different actions depending on the data that it is given. The command which tells the computer to do this is the IF command.

PRACTICAL EXERCISES

- -

Type

```
10 FOR AGE=8 TO 11
20    PRINT AGE;
30    PRINT
40 NEXT AGE
50 END
```

Did you notice the semi-colon at the end of Line 20? Now run the program. The output should be:

    8
    9
    10
    11

- -

The local football club runs a junior team called the under-10's. Only boys who are under 10 years of age are eligible to play. Let's get the computer to tell us the ages that can play for this team.

Modify the program to become:

```
10 FOR AGE=8 TO 11
20    PRINT AGE;
30    IF AGE<10 THEN PRINT " IS OK";
40    PRINT
50 NEXT AGE
60 END
```

and run the program. The output should be:

```
 8 IS OK
 9 IS OK
10
11
```

The '<' in Line 30 means <u>is less than</u>. Hence, Line 30 really means

> IF AGE is less than 10 THEN print 'IS OK' alongside the
>   age printed out by Line 20.

When AGE has a value of 8, then the condition AGE<10 is true (8 <u>is</u> less than 10), and so the message 'IS OK' is printed.

When AGE has a value of 9, then the condition AGE<10 is also true (9 <u>is</u> less than 10), and so the message 'IS OK' is printed.

When AGE has a value of 10, then the condition AGE<10 is false (10 is <u>not</u> less than 10, it is actually equal to 10), and so the message 'IS OK' is not printed.

When AGE has a value of 11, then the condition AGE<10 is again false (11 is <u>not</u> less than 10, it is actually greater than 10), and so the message 'IS OK' is not printed.

- -

The local school is organising a class outing. However, only children who are over 8 years of age can go, because it would be too tiring for younger children. Let's get the computer to tell us the ages that can go on this outing.

Modify Line 30 to become:

```
30 ..IF AGE>8 THEN PRINT " IS OK";
```

replacing the two dots by two spaces. Now run the program. The output should be:

```
8
9 IS OK
10 IS OK
11 IS OK
```

The '>' in Line 30 means is greater than. Hence, Line 30 really means:

> IF AGE is greater than 8 THEN print 'IS OK' alongside the
>   age printed out by Line 20.

Obviously, ages of 9, 10, and 11 satisfy this condition, because they are greater than 8, but an age of 8 does not.

- -

Load the POCKMONEY2 program from your UNIT PROGRAMS cassette. List and run the program, and make sure that it is working correctly. Now run it for ages of 10 and 11. The pocket money should be 50 pence for a 10-year old, and 55 pence for an 11-year old.

- -

We now want to modify the program so that any child who is more than 10 years of age (11, 12, and so on) receives an extra 20 pence in addition to his 5 pence for each year of his age.

Type

```
55 ..IF AGE>10 THEN PAY=PAY+20
```

List the program, and then run it for ages of 10 and 11. The pocket money should still be 50 pence for a 10-year old, but it should now be 75 pence for an 11-year old. Are your answers correct? If not, go back and check the program.

- -

10.2 What conditions can be tested?

Up to now, we have encountered TWO conditions:

<   meaning   'is less than'   e.g. IF AGE<10
>   meaning   'is greater than'   e.g. IF AGE>8

There are FOUR other conditions that are commonly used in BASIC:

=   meaning   'is equal to'
<>   meaning   'is not equal to'

<=   meaning   'is less than or equal to'
>=   meaning   'is greater than or equal to'

PRACTICAL EXERCISES

- -

A children's competition has been organised by the local library.
However, only 10-year olds can enter. Let's get the computer to
tell us the ages that can enter this competition.

Type
```
    NEW
    10 FOR AGE=8 TO 11
    20    PRINT AGE;
    30    IF AGE=10 THEN PRINT " IS OK";
    40    PRINT
    50 NEXT AGE
    60 END
```

and run the program. The '=' in Line 30 means is equal to. Is the
output what you would expect? The message 'IS OK' should only be
printed alongside an age of 10.

- -

For those children who were not eligible to enter the competition
the library has organised a film show.

Can you work out what ages (from 8, 9, 10, and 11-year olds) can
go to the film show?

Modify Line 30 to become:

```
    30 ..IF AGE<>10 THEN PRINT " IS OK";
```

and run the program. The '<>' in Line 30 means <u>is not equal to</u>.
If 10 is the only age that can enter the competition, then those
children who are NOT 10 (i.e. 8, 9, and 11-year olds) can go to
the film.

- -

A swimming club is entering a team for a swimming gala. One of
the age groups is '9 and under'. This means that only children
who are 9 or under 9 can be entered. Let's get the computer to
tell us the ages that can be entered in this age group.

Modify Line 30 to become:

        30 ..IF AGE<=9 THEN PRINT " IS OK";

and run the program. The '<=' in Line 30 means <u>is less than or
equal to.</u> Hence, Line 30 selects all children who are '9 or under
9'.

- -

Only children who are '10 or over' are allowed to take the
YOURTOWN cycling proficiency test. Let's get the computer to tell
us the ages that can take this test.

Modify Line 30 to become:

        30 ..IF AGE>=10 THEN PRINT " IS OK";

and run the program. The '>=' in Line 30 means <u>is greater than or
equal to.</u> Hence, Line 30 selects all children who are '10 or over
10'.

- -

```
******************************************************************
*                                                                *
*      <    means    'is less than'                              *
*      >    means    'is greater than'                           *
*                                                                *
*      =    means    'is equal to'                               *
*      <>   means    'is not equal to'                           *
*                                                                *
*      <=   means    'is less than or equal to'                  *
*      >=   means    'is greater than or equal to'               *
*                                                                *
******************************************************************
```

10.3 Using ELSE in an IF command

Up to now, all our decisions have been of the form:

    IF   some condition is true   THEN   take some action.

Occasionally, there are other actions which should be taken if the condition is NOT true. For example:

    IF   you are tired   THEN   go to bed
                      ELSE   read a book

The meaning should be obvious: if you are tired, then go to bed; otherwise you are not tired, so you can read a book. The BASIC on the BBC computer allows an ELSE to be included in the IF command. For example, we can modify our 'age' program to become (but don't type it yet):

```
10 FOR AGE=8 TO 11
20   PRINT AGE;
30   IF AGE>=10 THEN PRINT " IS OK";
              ELSE PRINT " IS NOT OK";
40   PRINT
50 NEXT AGE
60 END
```

If the condition AGE>=10 is true, the command following the THEN is executed. If the condition is not true, the command following the ELSE is executed. Hence, this program should display 'IS OK' alongside those ages which are greater than or equal to 10 (i.e. 10 and 11), and 'IS NOT OK' alongside those ages which are not greater than or equal to 10 (i.e. 8 and 9).

    As it is written, Line 30 is spread over two lines, and the ELSE part is positioned directly beneath the THEN part. This is done to make the command easy to read and simple to understand. Unfortunately, you cannot enter a command into the computer in this form. When you type Line 30 into the computer, you must type it as one long line. Using the AUTO command, you would type:

    ..IF AGE>=10 THEN PRINT " IS OK"; ELSE PRINT " IS NOT OK";

followed by the RETURN key. Replace the two dots by two spaces.

Do not press RETURN until you get to the end of the command.

As the screen is only 40 characters wide, this line is too long to fit on one line of the screen, and part will overflow onto the next line. It will appear on the screen as:

```
     30    IF AGE>=10 THEN PRINT " IS OK";
ELSE PRINT " IS NOT OK";
```

Even though it overflows to the next line on the screen, it is still treated <u>as one line</u> by BASIC. Indeed, one line of BASIC can contain up to 238 characters, which would occupy seven lines on the screen.

- -

Type this program into the computer. List it, and check that it is correct. In particular, look very carefully at Line 30. Now run the program. The output should be:

```
 8 IS NOT OK
 9 IS NOT OK
10 IS OK
11 IS OK
```

- -

One solution to Question 2 of Unit 9 is shown below.

Type
```
NEW
10 FOR K=1 TO 20
20    X=RND(2)
30    PRINT X
40 NEXT K
50 END
```

List your program, and check that you have typed it correctly. Now run the program. Is the output reasonable? There should be a random sequence of twenty 1's and 2's displayed on the screen.

- -

Now modify the program to become:

```
10 FOR K=1 TO 20
20    X=RND(2)
30    IF X=1 THEN PRINT "HEADS"
               ELSE PRINT "TAILS"
40 NEXT K
50 END
```

Did you remember to type Line 30 as one long line? When listed, it should appear on the screen as:

```
   30  IF X=1 THEN PRINT "HEADS" ELSE PR
INT "TAILS"
```

List your program, and check that you have typed it correctly.
Now run the program. Is the output reasonable? The output should
be a random sequence of twenty HEADS and TAILS.

- -

10.4 An example program

The following program plays a game called GUESS-THE-NUMBER. The
computer thinks of a number between 1 and 100, and you have to
guess it. The computer gives you clues as to whether your guess
is too large or too small.

```
 10 REM   GUESS-THE-NUMBER   (GUESSNUM1)
 20                                            c=0
 30 PRINT
 40 PRINT "THE COMPUTER WILL THINK OF"
 50 PRINT "A NUMBER BETWEEN 1 AND 100"
 60 PRINT
 70 PRINT "TRY TO GUESS IT"
 80 NUMBER=RND(100)
 90
100 REPEAT
110    PRINT
120    INPUT "ENTER GUESS ", GUESS
130                                            c=c+1
140    IF GUESS=NUMBER THEN 180
150
160    IF GUESS>NUMBER THEN PRINT "TOO LARGE"
                        ELSE PRINT "TOO SMALL"
170
180 UNTIL GUESS=NUMBER
190 PRINT CHR$(7); "WELL DONE"
200 END
```

A RND command is used in Line 80 to generate a random number in
the range 1..100. The program is basically just a REPEAT loop
(Lines 100–180). This loop is terminated when your GUESS is equal
to the computer's NUMBER. CHR$(7) in Line 190 simply rings the
bell inside the computer, to let you know that you have guessed
the number correctly. CHR$ is explained in Section 17.5, but at
this point we simply make use of it. Lines 20, 90, 130, 150, and
170 are included to break the program into sections, so as to
make it more readable. When you want to include a blank line,
press the SPACE bar once, and then press the RETURN key.

Line 140 shows the IF command being used differently. This version of the IF command has the form:

    IF some condition is true THEN transfer to a line-number.

Hence, the IF command in Line 140 tells the computer to transfer to Line 180 if GUESS is equal to NUMBER. If it is not, then the computer continues to the next line, which is Line 150.

- -

Type in the program. List it, and then check that you have typed it correctly. Now run the program. Does it work correctly? If not, go back and re-check, correcting any mistakes.

- -

When the program is correct, save it on your cassette as GUESSNUM1. Don't forget to fill in the 'cassette contents' sheet.

- -

```
*******************************************************************
*                                                                 *
*     There are three forms of the IF command:                    *
*                                                                 *
*          IF   condition   THEN   command                        *
*                                                                 *
*          IF   condition   THEN   command-1   ELSE   command-2    *
*                                                                 *
*          IF   condition   THEN   line-number                     *
*                                                                 *
*******************************************************************
```

10.5 Several commands on one line

Up to now, we have used only one command per line. You can, in fact, put several commands on a single line, so long as you separate the commands by colons.

Type

```
10 KSTART=5 : KFINISH=9
20 FOR K=KSTART TO KFINISH
30    PRINT K
40 NEXT K
50 END
```

and run the program. Does it produce the correct output? Notice
that there are two commands on Line 10, KSTART=5 and KFINISH=9.
These commands are separated by a colon (:).

In the examples of IF commands that we have used so far,
there has been only one command following the THEN and only one
command following the ELSE. However, you frequently need to have
more than one command either on the THEN branch, or on the ELSE
branch, or both. The following example is used in the next unit
(it must be typed as one long line, as described above):

```
IF X=1 THEN PRINT "HEADS" :
           ADDUP1=ADDUP1+1
      ELSE PRINT "TAILS" :
           ADDUP2=ADDUP2+1
```

There are TWO commands on the THEN branch (PRINT "HEADS" and
ADDUP1=ADDUP1+1). These commands are separated by a colon, and
will be executed if the condition X=1 is true.

There are TWO commands on the ELSE branch (PRINT "TAILS" and
ADDUP2=ADDUP2+1). These commands are separated by a colon, and
will be executed if the condition X=1 is not true.

There are times when you have to use several commands on one
line, especially with IF... THEN... ELSE commands. If at all
possible, however, you should avoid doing so, because it makes
programs difficult to read.

Questions

1.   What new commands have you met in this unit?

2.   What character or characters are used in BASIC to mean:

>   is less than?
>   is greater than?
>
>   is equal to?
>   is not equal to?
>
>   is less than or equal to?
>   is greater than or equal to?

3. Which condition would you use to test for ages:

    under 10?

    equal to 8?

    9 or under?

    over 10?

    10 or over?

    not 9?

4. For each of the conditions shown below, put a tick against each value of AGE which makes the condition true. The first has been done to show you what to do.

condition	AGE				
AGE<7	☑ 5	☑ 6	☐ 7	☐ 8	☐ 9
AGE>8	☐ 5	☐ 6	☐ 7	☐ 8	☐ 9
AGE<>7	☐ 5	☐ 6	☐ 7	☐ 8	☐ 9
AGE>=7	☐ 5	☐ 6	☐ 7	☐ 8	☐ 9
AGE=8	☐ 5	☐ 6	☐ 7	☐ 8	☐ 9
AGE<=8	☐ 5	☐ 6	☐ 7	☐ 8	☐ 9
AGE>3	☐ 5	☐ 6	☐ 7	☐ 8	☐ 9
AGE<5	☐ 5	☐ 6	☐ 7	☐ 8	☐ 9

5* In the following fragment of a program, will Line 40 or Line 70 be executed after Line 30?

```
10 A=17
20 B=8
30 IF A+B>25 THEN 70
40 ...
```

6*   In a match between two football teams, the team that plays on its own ground is called the HOME team, and the visitors are called the AWAY team.

If the HOME team wins the match, the result is a 'HOME win'.
If the AWAY team wins the match, the result is a 'AWAY win'.
If the scores are equal, the result is a 'DRAW'.

Write a program which will accept as input

a.   the number of goals scored by the HOME team
b.   the number of goals scored by the AWAY team

and then print the result of the match (HOME win, AWAY win or DRAW).

7*   The GUESS-THE-NUMBER program described in Section 10.4 can be simplified. Load GUESSNUM1 from your cassette, and modify it as follows:

    140 ..IF GUESS>NUMBER THEN PRINT "TOO LARGE"
    150 ..IF GUESS<NUMBER THEN PRINT "TOO SMALL"

    and delete Line 160

Run the program and check that it performs correctly. You should always examine your programs carefully after they are written, to see if they can be simplified.

11 Arrays

11.1 Arrays

In Unit 10 we developed a program to generate a random sequence of HEADS and TAILS. We now want to modify this program so that, in addition, it displays the number of HEADS and the number of TAILS that appear in the sequence.

```
10 ADDUP1=0
20 ADDUP2=0
30 FOR K=1 TO 20
40    X=RND(2)
50    IF X=1 THEN PRINT "HEADS" :
                    ADDUP1=ADDUP1+1
             ELSE PRINT "TAILS" :
                    ADDUP2=ADDUP2+1
60 NEXT K
70 PRINT
80 PRINT "THERE WERE "; ADDUP1; " HEADS"
90 PRINT "THERE WERE "; ADDUP2; " TAILS"
100 END
```

We introduce two new variables:

ADDUP1 to keep a count of the number of HEADS;
ADDUP2 to keep a count of the number of TAILS.

These variables are initially set to 0 in Lines 10 and 20. Within the FOR loop, ADDUP1 is increased by 1 in the THEN branch of Line 50 for each HEAD thrown, and ADDUP2 is increased by 1 in the ELSE branch of Line 50 for each TAIL thrown. When the loop is finished, the values in ADDUP1 and ADDUP2 are displayed by Lines 80 and 90.
When you come to type Line 50 into your computer, remember to type it as ONE line, and not as FOUR lines as shown here. When typed into the computer using AUTO, Line 50 should look like:

```
50    IF X=1 THEN PRINT "HEADS" : ADDU
P1=ADDUP1+1 ELSE PRINT "TAILS" : ADDUP2=
ADDUP2 + 1
```

Type this program into your computer. List it, and check that you
have typed it correctly. Now run the program - does it count the
HEADS and TAILS correctly? If not, re-check your program.

We can extend our Unit 9 DICE program in a similar way, using:

> ADDUP1 to count the number of 1's thrown;
> ADDUP2 to count the number of 2's thrown;
> ....
> ADDUP6 to count the number of 6's thrown.

The program is now getting quite long, because we need to test if
X is equal to 1, and, if so, add 1 to ADDUP1; then we need to
test if X is equal to 2, and, if so, add 1 to ADDUP2; and so on,
through to ADDUP6. A simpler method involves using 'arrays'.
   BASIC allows a number of memory boxes to be grouped under
ONE name. This group is called an array. The command

> DIM ADDUP(6)

tells the computer to group six boxes together, and call them
ADDUP. DIM is short for DIMension.

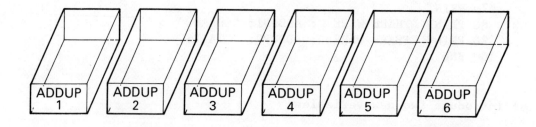

The first box of the array is Box 1, the second is Box 2, and so
on. In this example, the last box is Box 6, because the DIM
command specified that there were six boxes. An individual box is
selected by means of a subscript. The command

> LET ADDUP(3)=27

assigns the value 27 to the third box of ADDUP. The 3 is the
subscript, and it is written in brackets immediately after the
array name. The command

> LET X=ADDUP(3)

assigns to X the value that is currently held in the third box of
ADDUP (27 in this example).

PRACTICAL EXERCISES

- -

Type
```
     NEW
     DIM ADDUP(6)
     LET ADDUP(3)=27
     PRINT ADDUP(3)
```

The value held in the third box of ADDUP (27 in this example) is
displayed on the screen.

- -

Type

```
     LET X=ADDUP(3)
     PRINT X
```

The value currently held in Box 3 of ADDUP is assigned to X.

- -

Type

```
     PRINT ADDUP(4)
```

As yet, we have not assigned a value to the fourth box of ADDUP.
Some computers will tell you that you have made a mistake,
because a value has not been assigned. The BBC computer, however,
automatically sets all the boxes of an array to zero when the
computer executes the DIM command. Therefore, using an array box
to which you have not assigned a value is not an error, because
the computer has done it for you. Some computers don't set the
boxes of an array to zero (that is left for you to do in your
program), so be careful if you ever use such a computer.

- -

Type
```
     10 DIM ADDUP(6)
     20 FOR Al=1 TO 6
     30    ADDUP(Al)=10*Al
     40 NEXT Al
     50 END
     LIST
     RUN
```

This program defines an array ADDUP containing six memory boxes.
The FOR loop in Lines 20-40 sets the initial values in these
boxes to:

ADDUP

10	20	30	40	50	60
1	2	3	4	5	6

In this book, we adopt the following scheme for choosing the names of arrays and subscripts:

a)   All the names of arrays in a program should start with a different letter, e.g. ADDUP, SALES, PRICES.

b)   A variable used as a subscript to an array will have the same initial letter as the array, followed by a number, for example:

A1 is the subscript for the ADDUP array;
S1 is the subscript for the SALES array;
and so on.

If more than one subscript is needed for an array, then simply use the same initial letter, but another number, for example A2, A3.

- -

Type

PRINT ADDUP(6)

The value in the sixth box of ADDUP (i.e. 60) is displayed.

- -

Type

PRINT ADDUP(7)

The computer will display the error message 'Subscript' to tell you that you have made a mistake. There are only six boxes in the ADDUP array, yet you have tried to use Box 7, which doesn't exist.

- -

Type

PRINT ADDUP(-1)

Again, the computer will display the error message 'Subscript' to tell you that you have made a mistake, because the subscript is in error.

- -

Type

```
PRINT ADDUP(0)
```

Most computers will tell you that you have made a mistake, because the ADDUP boxes are numbered 1, 2,... 6, and you have tried to use Box 0. The BBC computer is an exception. The command DIM ADDUP(6) actually defines <u>seven</u> boxes in the BBC computer – these boxes are called Box 0, <u>Box</u> 1,... Box 6. Therefore, on the BBC computer, there actually is a Box 0. However, you are advised NOT to use this feature, because it can be confusing. Assume the boxes are numbered from 1 to the number of boxes you stated in the DIM command, and only use subscripts in this range.

- -

Type

```
PRINT PRICE(3)
```

The computer will display the error message 'Array' to tell you that you have made a mistake. You have not declared a PRICE array in a DIM command, and therefore it is a mistake to use the name PRICE with a subscript.

- -

```
********************************************************************
*                                                                  *
*     The command DIM X(10) declares an array called X, with       *
*     10 memory boxes.                                             *
*                                                                  *
*     These boxes are numbered 1, 2,... 10, therefore you          *
*     must only use subscripts in this range.                      *
*                                                                  *
********************************************************************
```

11.2 The DICE program

Let us now look at how we can use arrays in the DICE program to count the number of 1's, 2's, 3's, 4's, 5's and 6's we get when we throw a dice one hundred times.

```
10 REM DICE THROWING  (DICE1)
20 DIM ADDUP(6)
30
```

Line 20 declares an array called ADDUP, containing six boxes.

```
 40 FOR A1=1 TO 6
 50    ADDUP(A1)=0
 60 NEXT A1
 70
```

The FOR loop above sets each memory box of the ADDUP array to 0.

```
 80 FOR K=1 TO 100
 90    X=RND(6)
100    ADDUP(X)=ADDUP(X)+1
110 NEXT K
120
```

This FOR loop generates 100 random numbers in the range 1-6. On a given pass of the loop, the variable X holds the random number generated on that pass (for example, it could be 3). X is used as a subscript to the ADDUP array, and the box identified by ADDUP(X) (Box 3 in this example) has its value increased by 1. Hence, if Box 3 contained 10 at the start of this pass through the loop, then it would contain 11 at the finish of the pass. When the loop is finished:

    ADDUP(1) contains the number of 1's thrown;
    ADDUP(2) contains the number of 2's thrown;
       ...
    ADDUP(6) contains the number of 6's thrown;

The following loop displays the contents of each ADDUP box:

```
130 FOR A1=1 TO 6
140    PRINT A1;"   ";
150    PRINT ADDUP(A1)
160 NEXT A1
170
180 END
```

- -

Type NEW, and then enter this program into your computer. List it, and check that you have typed it correctly. Now run the program. Is it working correctly? If you add up the six numbers displayed on the screen, the total should be 100. If not, go back and re-check the program.

- -

When the program is correct, save it on your cassette as DICE1. Don't forget to fill in the 'cassette contents' sheet.

- -

11.3 Histograms

The output from the DICE program is a set of six numbers, for example:

```
1   16
2   23
3   14
4   18
5   15
6   14
```

The first number shows the numbers of 1's that appeared in one hundred throws of a dice; the second number shows the number of 2's that appeared; and so on. In this case, the ADDUP array is

```
ADDUP   | 16 | 23 | 14 | 18 | 15 | 14 |
           1    2    3    4    5    6
```

and the value in each box is displayed in turn by the commands:

```
130 FOR A1=1 TO 6
140    PRINT A1;"   ";
150    PRINT ADDUP(A1)
160 NEXT A1
```

Results are often more meaningful if they are displayed in a graphical form:

```
1   ****************
2   **********************
3   *************
4   *****************
5   ***************
6   *************
```

The number of asterisks in a line gives the number of times that the dice landed with that face upwards. For example, there are sixteen asterisks in Line 1 because there were 16 1's in the one hundred throws. This form of output is called a Histogram. This output will be produced if you replace Line 150 by the following lines. Replace the two dots (..) by two spaces so as to keep the correct indentation.

```
150 ..FOR J=1 TO ADDUP(A1)
151 ..   PRINT "*";
152 ..NEXT J
153 ..PRINT
```

If A1 is equal to 1, ADDUP(A1) contains 16. The FOR loop in Lines 150-152 is repeated 16 times, and an asterisk is printed each time. The semi-colon at the end of Line 151 ensures that all the asterisks are on the same line. Finally, when the loop is complete, the PRINT command in Line 153 moves the cursor to the beginning of the next line on the screen. This process is then repeated for the remaining boxes of ADDUP.

- -

Modify your DICE1 program as described above. List the program, and check that you have typed it correctly. Now run the program. Does it produce a histogram something like the one on the previous page? If not, correct your program, and re-run it.

- -

Modify Line 80 so that only 5 throws of the dice are made (i.e. change 100 to 5). Now run the program. The output should be something like

```
    1  *
    2  **
    3  *
    4  *
    5  **
    6  *
```

In particular, there will be at least one asterisk in every line. In this example, there are 8 asterisks in all. However, we only threw the dice 5 times, and so there should have been only 5 asterisks. Something is wrong!

- -

The problem arises when a box of the ADDUP array contains 0. In this case, Line 150 effectively becomes

```
    150 FOR J=1 TO 0
```

Unfortunately, on the BBC computer, the loop will be executed ONCE (printing an asterisk), and then the loop will be terminated because J now exceeds the final value (0). Hence, we get an asterisk on the screen even when the corresponding ADDUP box contains 0. The problem can be cured by inserting an IF command to bypass the loop whenever an ADDUP box contains 0.

Type
```
    145 ..IF ADDUP(A1)=0 THEN 153
```

Now run the program. There should now be only 5 asterisks.

- -

Renumber the program, modify the header to become (DICE2), and then save the program on your cassette as DICE2. Don't forget to fill in the 'cassette contents' sheet.

- -

Questions

1.   What new commands have you met in this unit?

2.   What is an array?

3.   What is a subscript?

4.   What scheme have we adopted in this book for naming arrays and subscripts?

5*   Write down a command which will define an array called MONTH containing 12 boxes.

6.   Write down a FOR loop which will set the values of all the MONTH boxes to 0.

7.   Write down a command which will increase the contents of the fifth MONTH box by 1.

8.   What will the command LET MONTH(3)=7 do?

9.   What will the command LET MONTH(13)=6 do?

10.   Write down a command which will define an array called ADDUP containing 6 boxes.

11.   Work out what values will be in the memory boxes after the computer has executed each of the following commands. Write your answers in the boxes provided.

ADDUP

7	3	4	6	8	1
1	2	3	4	5	6

ADDUP(3)=ADDUP(3)+1

ADDUP

1	2	3	4	5	6

ADDUP(6)=0

ADDUP

1	2	3	4	5	6

ADDUP(4)=ADDUP(5)/2

ADDUP

1	2	3	4	5	6

ADDUP(2)=9

ADDUP

1	2	3	4	5	6

ADDUP(5)=ADDUP(2)-ADDUP(3)

ADDUP

1	2	3	4	5	6

X=ADDUP(1)+3

ADDUP

1	2	3	4	5	6

ADDUP(4)=ADDUP(4)+ADDUP(3)

ADDUP

1	2	3	4	5	6

Now type each command into the computer in turn, and check (using PRINT commands after each one) that your answers are correct.

12 Example Program I

12.1 Background

There are three schools in YOURTOWN. These schools are called Arnside, Brookvale and Croft. The YOURTOWN cross-country running championships are held once a year, and these three schools each enter a team of five runners. Every runner wears a number on his vest. This number is used to identify both the runner, and the school to which he belongs. This is done by allocating

      Arnside   the numbers 1, 2, 3, 4, and 5;
      Brookvale the numbers 6, 7, 8, 9, and 10;
      Croft   the numbers 11, 12, 13, 14 and 15.

Hence, there are fifteen runners altogether (three teams each of five runners).

A marshal stands at the finishing post to record the positions in which the runners finish. This he does on a 'Race Record Sheet'.

```
POSITION   1 │  9 │
           2 │  3 │
           3 │ 14 │
           4 │    │
           5 │    │
           6 │    │
           7 │    │
           8 │    │
           9 │    │
          10 │    │
          11 │    │
          12 │    │
          13 │    │
          14 │    │
          15 │    │
```

When the first runner finishes, the marshal writes that runner's number in the box labelled POSITION 1. When the second runner finishes, he writes that runner's number in the box labelled POSITION 2. And so on, for all fifteen runners in the race. In this example, Runner 9 won the race, Runner 3 was second, and Runner 14 was third; the marshal is waiting for the fourth runner to finish.

When the race is over, and all the runners have finished, the marshal will analyse the results to determine which team has won. This analysis is done on the Race Record Sheet, as shown in Figure 12.1.

Firstly, the marshal works out the school to which each runner belongs, and writes the initial letter of the school in the SCHOOL column on the sheet. Runner 9 comes from Brookvale, so the marshal writes B in the SCHOOL column opposite POSITION 1. Runner 3 comes from Arnside, so the marshal writes A in the SCHOOL column opposite POSITION 2. And so on, for all fifteen runners.

The next step is to add up the positions of the five runners in each team. The marshal uses the three COUNT columns labelled A, B, and C on the Race Record Sheet to help him. First of all, he scans the SCHOOL column looking for the letter A. Whenever he finds an A, he writes the Position of that runner in the COUNT-A column. In this example, the Arnside runners finished in positions 2, 5, 9, 10, and 11. The marshal repeats the process for B and C; the Brookvale runners finished in positions 1, 4, 7, 8, and 12, while the Croft runners finished in positions 3, 6, 13, 14, and 15.

The final step is to add up the three COUNT columns. The totals are:

Arnside	37
Brookvale	32
Croft	51.

The winner is the school with the LOWEST overall total. This is because the fastest runner has a position of 1, whereas the slowest runner has a position of 15. Therefore, the smaller the position, the better the runner. Hence Brookvale school won the YOURTOWN cross-country running championships, Arnside were second and Croft were third.

Your task is to write a computer program to do the recording and the analysis of these results.

12.2 Designing the program

The marshal basically performs two tasks:

1.   during the race, he records the results, writing down the runner that finished in each position;

RACE RECORD SHEET   September 1984

POSITION	SCHOOL	COUNT		
		A	B	C
1	9	B		1	
2	3	A	2		
3	14	C			3
4	7	B		4	
5	1	A	5		
6	15	C			6
7	8	B		7	
8	10	B		8	
9	2	A	9		
10	5	A	10		
11	4	A	11		
12	6	B		12	
13	11	C			13
14	13	C			14
15	12	C			15
TOTALS		37	32	51

Winner   : Brookvale
Runner-up : Arnside
Third   : Croft

Figure 12.1: The Race Record Sheet for the YOURTOWN cross-country running championships.

2.   after the race is over, he analyses the results to find
out which team has won.

Let us similarly split our program into two parts, and consider
each part separately.

12.2.1 Recording the results

We can record the results in the computer in a way which is
similar to the way the marshal recorded the results on the Race
Record Sheet. If we define an array called POSITION with 15
memory boxes, then we can record in each box the number of the
runner who finished in that position.

```
10 REM CROSS-COUNTRY PROGRAM (CROSS1)
20 DIM POSITION(15)
```

This is version 1 of the cross-country program. Now we need a
loop repeatedly to ask the marshal to enter the numbers of the
runners as they finish. As we know there will be exactly 15
runners, we should use a FOR loop in preference to a REPEAT loop.

```
 30
 40 REM   RECORD THE RESULTS
 50
 60 FOR P1=1 TO 15
 70    PRINT
 80    PRINT "POSITION ";P1;
 90    INPUT "  RUNNER ",RUNNER
100    POSITION(P1)=RUNNER
110 NEXT P1
120 PRINT
```

The loop is repeated 15 times, and the marshal is asked to enter
the runner who finished in each position. The loop control
variable P1 is used as the subscript to the POSITION array.
    Let us now print out the POSITION array so that we can check
that the information has been entered correctly.

```
130
140 REM   CHECK THE DATA
150
160 FOR P1=1 TO 15
170    PRINT "POSITION ";P1;
180    PRINT "  RUNNER ";POSITION(P1)
190 NEXT P1
200 PRINT
```

This group of commands is put into the program simply to check
that the program is correct up to this point. If the data is
printed correctly here, then it gives us confidence that the
program is correct so far. These are called <u>testing statements</u>,
because their purpose is to test the program, and satisfy us that
the program is working correctly. When the program is complete,
the 'testing statements' will be removed.

PRACTICAL EXERCISES

- -

Type this program into your computer. List it, and then run it
for the finishing positions shown in Figure 12.1 (Runner 9 first,
Runner 3 second,... Runner 12 last). Does the program work
correctly? If not, go back and correct it.

- -

When the program is working correctly, save it on your cassette
as CROSS1.

- -

12.2.2 Analysing the results

The second part of the program analyses the data recorded in the
POSITION array, and determines which team has won. We need to
determine the school to which each runner belongs. At this point
in the book we do not yet know how to use letters within a
program (e.g. A for Arnside). Therefore, we will use team numbers
instead:

   Team 1 is Arnside;
   Team 2 is Brookvale;
   Team 3 is Croft.

We can find out the 'team number' that a particular runner
belongs to by using the command:

   LET TEAM=1 + (RUNNER-1) DIV 5

At this stage you will not understand precisely how this command
works. It will be explained in Unit 20. However, you should
satisfy yourself that it does indeed work correctly.

Type

```
NEW
10 FOR RUNNER=1 TO 15
20    TEAM=1 + (RUNNER-1) DIV 5
30    PRINT RUNNER, TEAM
40 NEXT RUNNER
50 END
```

List and run the program. The output should show that Runners 1-5 belong to Team 1, Runners 6-10 belong to Team 2, and Runners 11-15 belong to Team 3. This is just a rough-and-ready program whose purpose is simply to demonstrate that the command

```
LET TEAM=1 + (RUNNER-1) DIV 5
```

works correctly. When you are satisfied that it does, you can discard the program. This sort of program is often called a throw-away program. There is no point in spending a lot of effort in making such a program neat and tidy, because you are going to discard the program anyway, when its purpose has been served,
    Now we want to add up the positions of the runners in each team. One way is to scan the POSITION array, extracting each runner in turn. We can work out the runner's team, and then add the position to that team's COUNT. This process is then repeated for all runners. A more precise description is:


```
loop for each box in the POSITION array
     get runner
     determine the runner's team
     add the position to that team's COUNT
end loop
```


This form of English is often called Structured English. It provides a precise means of specifying what you require a program to do. Now we must translate this specification into BASIC. We first need to declare a COUNT array containing 3 boxes, one for each of the teams. We can simply change Line 20:

```
20 DIM POSITION(15), CNT(3)
```

We have used CNT instead of COUNT because COUNT is a reserved word on the BBC computer. In this situation, you can either choose another name (e.g. ADDUP), or abbreviate the name - as we have done here. Translated into BASIC, the specification becomes:

```
210
220 REM   CALCULATE THE TEAM TOTALS
230
240 FOR P1=1 TO 15
  250   RUNNER=POSITION(P1)
  260   TEAM=1 + (RUNNER-1) DIV 5
  270   PRINT "RUNNER ";RUNNER;
  280   PRINT "  TEAM ";TEAM
  290   CNT(TEAM)=CNT(TEAM)+P1
300 NEXT P1
```

Lines 270 and 280 are testing statements. Again, they have been inserted so that you can satisfy yourself that the program is working correctly.

Finally, the program should display each team's count on the screen.

```
310
320 REM   DISPLAY THE RESULTS
330
340 FOR TEAM=1 TO 3
  350   PRINT "TEAM ";TEAM;"    ";CNT(TEAM)
360 NEXT TEAM
370
380 END
```

PRACTICAL EXERCISES

- -

Load CROSS1 from your cassette. List it and run it, and make sure that it is working correctly.

- -

Edit Lines 10 and 20 to become:

```
10 REM CROSS-COUNTRY PROGRAM (CROSS2)
20 DIM POSITION(15), CNT(3)
```

Notice that we have changed the program heading to become CROSS2. When we have finished extending the program, we will store it on cassette under the name CROSS2.

- -

Add Lines 210-380 as shown above. List the program, and check that it is correct. Now run the program with the finishing positions shown in Figure 12.1 (Runner 9 first, Runner 3 second,... Runner 12 last). Does the program perform correctly? If not, go back and correct it.

- -

12.3 Testing the program

We have tried the program with one set of data, and the program SEEMS to be working correctly. We reached this conclusion because the answers produced by the program agree with the answers shown in Figure 12.1, which were obtained by processing the data by hand.

There is an additional check we can carry out. As there are only 15 runners, there can be only 15 finishing positions, ranging from 1 to 15. Adding these positions together, we get:

1+2+3+4+5+6+7+8+9+10+11+12+13+14+15 = 120

When there are three teams, then five of the positions go to Team 1, five go to Team 2, and five go to Team 3. Hence, the three teams account for all 15 positions. Therefore, the three team totals added together should also give a total of 120. Team 1 scored 37, Team 2 scored 32 and Team 3 scored 51, therefore the total is

37+32+51 = 120

The total is as expected.

We will have more confidence in the program if it works correctly for other sets of data.

PRACTICAL EXERCISES

- -

Process the following data by hand:

POSITION	1	2	3	4	5	6	7	8	9	10	11	12	13	14	15
RUNNER	1	2	3	4	5	6	7	8	9	10	11	12	13	14	15

Now run the program with this data. Does it produce the same answers as you obtained by hand?

- -

Process the following data by hand:

POSITION	1	2	3	4	5	6	7	8	9	10	11	12	13	14	15
RUNNER	6	1	11	7	2	12	8	3	13	14	4	15	9	5	10

Now run the program with this data. Does it produce the same answers as you obtained by hand?

— —

Process the following data by hand:

POSITION	1	2	3	4	5	6	7	8	9	10	11	12	13	14	15
RUNNER	16	11	21	17	12	22	18	13	23	24	14	25	19	15	20

Now run the program with this data. Does it produce the same answers as you obtained by hand? The computer will tell you that there is an error in the program. This arises because runners should have a number between 1 and 15, yet you have tried to enter numbers such as 16, 21, 25, and so on. Our testing has revealed a <u>fault</u> in the program. We must now modify the program to eliminate this fault. These modifications are described in Section 12.4.

— —

The program seems to work correctly so long as it is given valid data. Therefore, we can now delete the 'testing statements'.

Type

```
DELETE 130,200
DELETE 270,280
```

List the program, and run it with the data shown in Figure 12.1. Is the output correct? If not, go back and correct the program.

— —

Type
```
RENUMBER
LIST
```

Your program should now be the same as the program shown at the top of the next page. If it is different, then edit your program to be the same. Now save the program on your cassette as CROSS2.

— —

```
 10 REM CROSS-COUNTRY PROGRAM (CROSS2)
 20 DIM POSITION(15), CNT(3)
 30
 40 REM  RECORD THE RESULTS
 50
 60 FOR Pl=1 TO 15
 70   PRINT
 80   PRINT "POSITION ";Pl;
 90   INPUT "  RUNNER ",RUNNER
100   POSITION(Pl)=RUNNER
110 NEXT Pl
120 PRINT
130
140 REM  CALCULATE THE TEAM TOTALS
150
160 FOR Pl=1 TO 15
170   RUNNER=POSITION(Pl)
180   TEAM=1 + (RUNNER-1) DIV 5
190   CNT(TEAM)=CNT(TEAM)+Pl
200 NEXT Pl
210
220 REM  DISPLAY THE RESULTS
230
240 FOR TEAM=1 TO 3
250   PRINT "TEAM ";TEAM;"    ";CNT(TEAM)
260 NEXT TEAM
270
280 END
```

12.4 Modifying the program

In this section, you will see how to modify your program to make
it only accept numbers between 1 and 15. The portion of the
program that needs modifying is:

```
 60 FOR Pl=1 TO 15
 70   PRINT
 80   PRINT "POSITION ";Pl;
 90   INPUT "  RUNNER ",RUNNER
100   POSITION(Pl)=RUNNER
110 NEXT Pl
```

Line 90 accepts the number entered by the marshal, and Line 100
stores this number in the POSITION array. We need to insert some
commands to check whether the number is valid. If it is, Line 100
should be executed, otherwise the computer should display an
error message, and then ask the marshal to re-enter the number.

PRACTICAL EXERCISES

- -

Load CROSS2 from your cassette. List it, and run it to make sure
it is working correctly.

- -

Renumber the program so that there are plenty of spare line-
numbers at the point where the insertions are to be made.

Type
        RENUMBER 100,100
        LIST

The line-numbers now increase in steps of 100, and our insertions
will be made between Line 900 and Line 1000.

- -

Let us number our new lines in steps of 5, starting at 905. The
command AUTO 905,5 will do this. In the following commands, type
the two dots (..) as two spaces.

Type
        905 ..
        910 ..IF RUNNER<1 THEN
                PRINT "NUMBER IS LESS THAN 1" :
                GOTO 700
        915 ..
        920 ..IF RUNNER>15 THEN
                PRINT "NUMBER IS GREATER THAN 15" :
                GOTO 700
        925 ..

        990 ..PRINT "ACCEPTED"

We have inserted two commands. The first command (Line 910)
checks whether the number is less than 1. If it is, an error
message is displayed (by the PRINT command), and control is sent
back (by the GOTO 700 command) to Line 700, where the computer
asks the marshal to enter the number again. If the number is NOT
less than 1, the computer passes on to the second command.
        The second command (Line 920) checks whether the number is
greater than 15. If it is, an error message is displayed (by the
PRINT command), and control is sent back (by the GOTO 700
command) to Line 700, where the computer asks the marshal to
enter the number again. If the number is NOT greater than 15,
then the number must be in the range 1..15, and so the computer

passes on to Line 990, which displays ACCEPTED on the screen. Hereafter, the program is exactly the same as before.

We have introduced a new command: the GOTO command. The format of this command is 'GOTO line-number'. Its purpose is exactly what you would expect - to send control to the nominated line. It is often called an <u>unconditional branch</u> because it causes the computer to branch out of its normal path of executing the command immediately following the current command. Contrast this with the 'IF condition THEN line-number' command, which is called a <u>conditional branch</u> because the branch to the line-number is taken only if the condition is true.

- -

List the program, and run it with the data given in Figure 12.1. Whilst entering numbers, try number 0 and number 16. They should both be rejected. If they are not, then go back and correct the program.

- -

When the program is working correctly, save it on your cassette as CROSS3.

- -

Questions

1* Load CROSS3 from your cassette. List it, and then run it to make sure that it is working correctly. Now run it with the following data:

        1 1 1 1   1 1 1 1   1 1 1 1

The program should accept this data, and produce an answer. The answer is obviously meaningless because you have entered the same runner fifteen times. We have found another fault in the program, namely that before accepting a runner it doesn't check to see if that runner has been entered previously. Your task is to eliminate this fault from the program.

We need to insert another group of commands between Line 925 and Line 990 to check whether the number has been entered before. If it has, the computer should display an error message, and then ask the marshal to re-enter the number. Otherwise, the computer should pass on to Line 990.

Outline Solution

a)   Declare an array with 15 boxes called USED. Remember
      that the boxes of an array are set to 0 automatically.

b)   Whenever a runner is accepted, set USED(RUNNER) to 1.

c)   Before accepting a runner, check whether USED(RUNNER)
      is equal to 1. If it is, then that number has been used
      before.

Modify your CROSS3 program as shown above. List it, and then run
it with the data given in Figure 12.1. Whilst entering the data,
try one or two numbers which you have already entered. These
should be rejected. If they are not, then go back and correct the
program. Save the program on your cassette as CROSS4.

2.   As question 1, but using a different solution. Suppose the
marshal has entered three runners (Runner 9, Runner 3 and Runner
14), and the computer is waiting for the marshal to enter the
fourth runner. The POSITION boxes will contain:

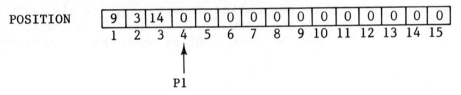

At this point, P1 contains 4. When the fourth runner is entered,
we can scan the boxes from 1 to P1 to see if our new RUNNER value
is in one of them. If it is, then we should reject that number.

Type
```
930 ..WRONG=0
935 ..FOR P2=1 TO P1
940 ..   IF POSITION(P2)=RUNNER THEN WRONG=1 : P2=P1
945 ..NEXT P2
950 ..IF WRONG=1 THEN PRINT "NUMBER ALREADY USED" : GOTO 700
955 ..
```

Notice that we are using another loop control variable (P2) which
we vary from 1 to P1. If any POSITION(P2) is equal to RUNNER,
then that number has been used before, and we reject it.
      Modify your CROSS3 program as shown above. List it, and then
run it with the data given in Figure 12.1. Whilst entering the
data, try one or two numbers which you have already entered.
These should be rejected. If they are not, then go back and
correct the program. Save the program on your cassette as CROSS5.

13 Developing a program

13.1 Introduction

In the previous unit we developed a computer program to record
and analyse the results of a cross-country running championship.
In this unit, we will be examining the various phases involved in
developing such a program. In essence, the development of a
program can be divided into three distinct phases:

analysis : when you decide WHAT is required;
design : when you decide HOW the program is to be
constructed;
construction : when you actually write the program in BASIC.
The testing of the program, and the
elimination of faults when they are detected
(often called debugging), are also included
in the construction phase. Hence construction
can be thought of as programming, testing and
debugging.

13.2 The Analysis Phase

It is during the Analysis Phase that you decide WHAT is required
of the program. Taking the cross-country program as an example,
we decided at some point that the program should be able to
record the finishing positions of the runners as they were
entered by the marshal, and, when all the runners had finished,
to work out the total scores gained by each school. There are
other things that the program COULD have done, for example,
answering the questions:

Who came sixth?
What position was JOHN SMITH?

but we decided that these questions (along with many other
things) were outside the scope of the program. Hence, by the end
of the Analysis Phase, you should be able to write down a set of
Requirements stating exactly what the program should be able to
do. These Requirements define the scope of the program. The
Requirements for the cross-country program might have been:

1. The program need only work for the three schools in YOURTOWN. It is not intended to be a general purpose program capable of being used at ANY cross-country running championship.
2. Using the keyboard, the marshal must be able to enter the number of the runner who finished in each position.
3. The program must be able to recognise mistakes made by the marshal, and act appropriately.
4. The program must be able to display the totals of the finishing positions scored by all three schools.
5. The program must be easy to use.

13.3 The Design Phase

It is during the Design Phase that you decide HOW the program is going to be constructed so that it will satisfy the Requirements identified in the Analysis Phase. For example, in the cross-country program, we decided that it was necessary to keep within the program a record of the runner who finished in each position. This was done using an array (which we called POSITION) with 15 memory boxes. When a runner's number is entered by the marshal, it is stored in the appropriate POSITION box. This is repeated for all fifteen runners.

We commence the Design Phase with the Requirements. Working from these Requirements, we can produce an outline specification of the program. The next step is to add more detail to this outline to give a more detailed specification. This latest specification is further refined by yet another step, and so on, until we have a specification which is sufficiently detailed to allow the program to be written. This process is called step-wise refinement, because we proceed in steps, refining the previous step by adding more detail. This process was used in Unit 12 to develop the cross-country program.

There are often several ways of doing something. For example, two methods are described in the questions at the end of Unit 12 for checking whether a runner has been entered before. When this situation arises, you must weigh up the alternatives, and select the best method.

The end-product of the Design Phase is the Program Specification. For a simple program such as the one developed in Unit 12, the Program Specification may only be a few notes describing the POSITION array, and how it is to be used. For more complex programs, such as the one developed in Unit 30, the Program Specification will be more detailed. Indeed, it may even be written in a special language used solely for designing programs. One such language is Structured English, which is described in detail in 'Software Engineering for Small Computers' by R. B. Coats, published by Edward Arnold. At this point of the book, however, we are only concerned with relatively simple programs, and so the Program Specifications are themselves simple.

13.4 The Construction Phase

It is during the Construction Phase that you write the program in BASIC, as per the Program Specification. This process is called Programming (sometimes Coding). When the program is written, it must be tested to check that it meets all the Requirements. If it doesn't, then there are faults in the program. These faults are often called bugs, and the process of removing them is called debugging. Testing and debugging are described in Unit 29. The remainder of this section describes programming.

```
 10 REM CROSS-COUNTRY PROGRAM (CROSS2)
 20 DIM POSITION(15), CNT(3)
 30
 40 REM   RECORD THE RESULTS
 50
 60 FOR P1=1 TO 15
 70    PRINT
 80    PRINT "POSITION ";P1;
 90    INPUT "  RUNNER ",RUNNER
100    POSITION(P1)=RUNNER
110 NEXT P1
120 PRINT
130
140 REM   CALCULATE THE TEAM TOTALS
150
160 FOR P1=1 TO 15
170    RUNNER=POSITION(P1)
180    TEAM=1 + (RUNNER-1) DIV 5
190    CNT(TEAM)=CNT(TEAM)+P1
200 NEXT P1
210
220 REM   DISPLAY THE RESULTS
230
240 FOR TEAM=1 TO 3
250    PRINT "TEAM ";TEAM;"    ";CNT(TEAM)
260 NEXT TEAM
270
280 END
```

It is important that your programs are easy to understand. A crucial factor in this respect is the layout of a program. This is concerned with organising the commands within the program, and is best explained by example. The following points relate to the program shown opposite.

Program Header. Every program should have a Header giving a title to the program, and showing the name under which this program is saved on cassette.

Groups of commands. The commands within a program can usually be divided into groups, each with a specific purpose. For example:

    Lines 60-120 are concerned with 'recording the results';
    Lines 160-200 are concerned with 'calculating the totals';
    Lines 240-260 are concerned with 'displaying the results'.

Group Headers. Each group of commands should be preceded by a Remark explaining the purpose of that group. Line 40, Line 140 and Line 220 are the Group Headers in this program. These Headers have a blank line before and after, so as to make them stand out, thus emphasising the structure of the program.

Line numbers. Line numbers should increase in uniform steps, for example 10, 20, 30, and so on. You should always RENUMBER your program after you have inserted or deleted lines.

Meaningful variable names. Programs are easier to understand if you use meaningful variable names. For example, names like TEAM and POSITION convey to the reader the purpose of these variables.

Indentation. This is a particularly important method of improving the clarity of your program. For example, Lines 70-100 are indented by two spaces to emphasise that they belong to, and are controlled by, the FOR loop beginning at Line 60.

Throw-away programs. A throw-away program is a rough-and-ready program whose purpose is to improve your understanding of some feature of the BASIC or the computer that you are using. For example, in Unit 12, you wrote a small program to satisfy yourself that the command

    LET TEAM=1 + (RUNNER-1) DIV 5

worked correctly. When you are satisfied, you can simply discard the program because it has served its purpose. Experimenting like this is a very valuable way of increasing your understanding of your computer.

Questions

1.   What are the three phases of program development?

2.   Describe what is done in each phase.

3.   What are the end-products of each phase?

4.   What is meant by programming?

5.   Why is program layout important?

6*   If you study the 'cross-country' program carefully, you will discover that the POSITION array is needed only to check whether a runner has already been entered. Rewrite the program, but miss out the POSITION array (assume that only correct data will be entered).

Hint: perhaps you can 'calculate the team totals' at the same time as you 'read the results'.

7*   Write a program to produce a histogram of the months in which the birthdays of a group of children fall. The program should cater for up to 30 children. The output should be like:

```
 1 *
 2 **
 3 **
 4
 5 *****
 6 **
 7 ***
 8 *
 9 ***
10 *****
11 *
12 ***
```

In this example, there was one child born in January, two born in February, two born on March, none in April, and so on. There were 28 children in the group (because there are 28 asterisks altogether). An outline of the program is shown on the next page:

```
define an ADDUP array with 12 memory boxes

ask the user to enter the NUMBER of children in the group
if NUMBER is less than 1 ask again
if NUMBER is greater than 30 ask again

for K=1 to NUMBER

    ask the user to enter the MONTH (1-12) of this birthday
    if MONTH is less than 1 ask again
    if MONTH is greater than 12 ask again

    add one to ADDUP(MONTH)

next K

display the histogram
end
```

Save the program on your cassette as BIRTHDAY1.

14 Nested loops

We have met REPEAT loops in Unit 7 and FOR loops in Unit 8. In this unit, we will see how we can use loops within loops.

- -

Load TABLES1 from your UNIT PROGRAMS cassette. List and run it, to make sure that it is working correctly.

- -

Modify the program to become:

```
 10 REM  TABLES PROGRAM  (TABLES2)
 20
 30 REPEAT
 40    INPUT "WHICH TABLE ",TABLE
 50    FOR K=1 TO 10
 60       ANSWER=K*TABLE
 70       PRINT K;" TIMES ";TABLE;" = ";ANSWER
 80    NEXT K
 90    PRINT
100 UNTIL TABLE=0
110 END
```

Run the program for several values of table. We have extended our original program by putting a REPEAT loop around the group of commands which produce the table. Now the computer will generate tables over and over again, until we stop it by entering a table value of 0. Our program now has the following structure:

REPEAT

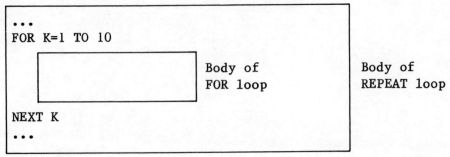

UNTIL TABLE=0

The body of the REPEAT loop now contains a FOR loop. The FOR loop is said to be <u>nested</u>, because it is inside another loop. Nested loops are often called <u>inner</u> loops, because they are INSIDE an <u>outer</u> loop.

Indentation is particularly important with nested loops. Lines 40, 50, 80 and 90 are indented by the normal TWO spaces. Because Lines 60 and 70 are the body of the nested loop, they are indented by a further TWO spaces, making a total indentation of FOUR spaces.

- -

When the program is working correctly, save it on your cassette as TABLES2. Don't forget to fill in the 'cassette contents' sheet.

- -

In the following example, a FOR loop is nested inside another FOR loop.

Type

```
NEW
10 FOR J=1 TO 2
20   PRINT "J = ";J
30   FOR K=1 TO 3
40     PRINT "K = ";K
50   NEXT K
60   PRINT
70 NEXT J
80 END
```

List the program, and check that you have typed it correctly. Now run the program. The output should be:

```
J = 1
K = 1
K = 2
K = 3

J = 2
K = 1
K = 2
K = 3
```

The J loop is the 'outer' loop and the K loop is the 'inner' loop. The program works as follows:

Line 10   : J is set to 1.
Line 20   : prints the value in J.

Lines 30-50 :   This FOR loop is executed THREE times, with K
                 values of 1, 2 and 3. The value in K is printed on
                 each execution of the loop.
Line 60   :   prints a blank line.
Line 70   :   J is increased by 1, so J becomes 2.

The J loop is now performed again. Notice that for EACH value of
J, the K loop is performed THREE times; this is because the K
loop is inside the J loop.

- -

Modify the program to become:

```
10 FOR J=1 TO 2
20    PRINT "J = ";J
30    FOR K=1 TO 3
40       PRINT "K = ";K
50    NEXT J
60    PRINT
70 NEXT K
80 END
```

List the program, and check that you have typed it correctly.
Notice that Line 50 has become NEXT J, and that Line 70 has
become NEXT K. Now run the program. The output will be:

```
J = 1
K = 1
J = 2
K = 1
```

and then the computer will display the error message 'No FOR at
line 70'. It may not be obvious what this message means. The
problem is that the NEXT K command has been placed after the NEXT
J command, and so the body of the K loop overlaps the body of the
J loop. This is not allowed: an inner loop must be totally inside
an outer loop.

FOR J=1 TO 2

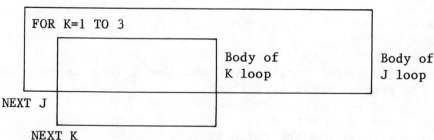

         Body of   Body of
         K loop   J loop

```
**************************************************************
*                                                          *
*     The body of an inner loop must be completely inside the  *
*     body of the outer loop.                              *
*                                                          *
**************************************************************
```

- -

Modify the program to become:

```
10 FOR J=1 TO 10
20    FOR K=1 TO 3
30       PRINT J*K;
40    NEXT K
50    PRINT
60 NEXT J
70 END
```

and run the program. The output should be:

1	2	3
2	4	6
3	6	9
.	.	.
10	20	30

This is simply a table of 'tables'. The program works as follows:

Line 10   : J is set to 1
Lines 20-40 : This FOR loop is executed THREE times, with K
                values of 1, 2 and 3. The result of multiplying J
                by K is printed on EACH execution of the loop. The
                semicolon at the end of Line 30 ensures that the
                three values are displayed on the same line.
Line 50   : moves the cursor to the start of the next line.
Line 60   : J is increased by 1, so J becomes 2.

The J loop is now performed TEN times. For EACH value of J, the K
loop is performed THREE times; this is because the K loop is
inside the J loop.

- -

Questions

1.   What is a <u>nested</u> loop?

2.   What are <u>inner</u> and <u>outer</u> loops?

3.   Why is indentation particularly important with nested loops?

4.   Rewrite the following program using proper indentation:

```
10 FOR A=1 TO 3
20 PRINT "A = ";A
30 FOR B=1 TO 5
40 PRINT "B = ";B
50 NEXT B
60 PRINT
70 NEXT A
80 END
```

5.   What output will the previous program produce? Type the program into your computer, and run it. Is the output as you expect?

6.   What output will the following program produce?

```
10 FOR A=1 TO 3
20    PRINT "A = ";A
30    FOR B=A TO 5
40       PRINT "B = ";B
50    NEXT B
60    PRINT
70 NEXT A
80 END
```

Type the program into your computer, and run it. Is the output as you expect?

7*   Modify the TABLES2 program so that it terminates as soon as you enter a table value of 0, and does not display the zero times table.

15 Strings

15.1 Strings and string variables

In previous units we have used the PRINT command to display messages on the screen. For example

    PRINT "POCKET MONEY = "

will display the message POCKET MONEY = on the screen. The set of characters between the quotes is called a <u>string</u>. A <u>character</u> is any of the symbols on the keys of the keyboard. This includes:

the capital letters	A, B, C,... Z
the small letters	a, b, c,... z
the numbers	1, 2, 3,... 9
a space	
the special characters	<, >, ?, $,%,...

Note that a space is counted as a character. Hence, there are 15 characters in the string "POCKET MONEY = " (11 letters, 3 spaces and an =). Because the quote character(") is used to mark the beginning and the end of a string, there are difficulties in using it as a character within the string; at this stage you are advised to avoid doing so. A string may contain no characters at all. This is called a <u>null string</u>, and it is written as "". The string " " contains a single space between the quotes, and is NOT the same as the null string.

The command LET AGE=10 defines a memory box called AGE, and stores the number 10 in it. This memory box is really a 'number' memory box because it is used to hold numbers. Strings can be stored in memory just as we can store numbers in memory.

The command

    LET WORD$="COMPUTER"

defines a 'string' memory box called WORD$, and stores the string "COMPUTER" in it.

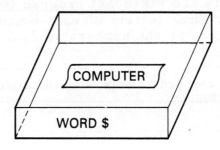

The $ at the end of the variable name tells the computer that this is a <u>string variable</u> which is to be used to hold strings. There is usually a maximum length of string that the computer can deal with. On the BBC computer it is 255 characters.

15.2 Arrays of strings

You can declare an array of memory boxes to hold strings just as you can declare an array of memory boxes to hold numbers. For example, the command

        10 DIM MONTH$(12)

declares a string array called MONTH$ with 12 memory boxes. Each box can hold one string. Strings can be assigned to the boxes in the usual way:

        20 MONTH$(1)="JAN"
        30 MONTH$(2)="FEB"
        .. ...
        130 MONTH$(12)="DEC"

PRACTICAL EXERCISES
- -
Type Lines 10–130 into your computer. Then type

        140
        150 FOR K=1 TO 12
        160   PRINT MONTH$(K)
        170 NEXT K
        180 END

and run the program. Check that it performs correctly.

- -

Modify the BIRTHDAY1 program (Question 7, Unit 13) so that the first three letters of each month are printed with the histogram, in place of the numbers 1, 2,... 12.

- -

When the program is working correctly, save it on your cassette as BIRTHDAY2.

- -

15.3 Manipulating strings

To manipulate strings, BASIC provides what are called <u>functions</u>. We deal with functions later, in Unit 21, but at this stage we can simply make use of them. The more common string functions are described below.

15.3.1 Length of a string

The length of a string is defined as the number of characters between the quotes. Hence, the length of the string "TELEVISION" is 10, and the length of the null string is 0. The LEN function is used in BASIC to determine the length of a string.

Type

```
10 A$="POCKET MONEY = "
20 PRINT "LENGTH OF A$ IS "; LEN(A$)
30 B$="ABCDE"
40 PRINT "LENGTH OF B$ IS "; LEN(B$)
50 C$=""
60 PRINT "LENGTH OF C$ IS "; LEN(C$)
70 D$=" "
80 PRINT "LENGTH OF D$ IS "; LEN(D$)
90 END
```

LEN(A$) tells the computer to count how many characters there are in the string A$. Now run the program. Are the answers as you expect? Notice that the length of C$ is 0 because it is a null string, but that the length of D$ is 1 because it contains a single space.

15.3.2 Concatenation of strings

<u>Concatenation</u> is the name given to the operation of joining two strings together to form one long string.

Type

```
10 GAME$="FOOT"+"BALL"
20 PRINT GAME$
30 END
```

Run the program. The output should be FOOTBALL. When a + sign is placed between two strings ("FOOT" and "BALL" in this example), the computer will join the two strings together to form one long string ("FOOTBALL"). Strings held in string variables can also be concatenated (e.g. A$=B$+C$).

15.3.3 Substrings

Concatenation combines strings together to form longer strings. However, you often want to do the opposite - to break a string up into parts. A substring is a sequence of consecutive characters within a string. For example "DEF" is a substring of the string "ABCDEFGHIJ". BASIC commonly provides three functions to help you extract substrings.

LEFT$(X$,N)   tells the computer to extract the substring made up of the left-most N characters of X$.

RIGHT$(X$,N)   tells the computer to extract the substring made up of the right-most N characters of X$.

MID$(X$,M,N)   tells the computer to extract the substring made up of N characters of X$, starting at the M'th character position.

- -

Type
```
10 X$="ABCDEFGHIJ"                                    ABCDEFGHIJ

20 PRINT LEFT$(X$,3)                                  ABCDEFGHIJ

30 PRINT RIGHT$(X$,4)                                 ABCDEFGHIJ

40 PRINT MID$(X$,4,3)                                 ABCDEFGHIJ

50 END
```

Run the program. The substrings printed out should be the same as those shown underlined on the right of the commands.

- -

Type
```
10 X$="ABCDEFGHIJ"
20 REPEAT
30    INPUT "ENTER M ",M
40    INPUT "ENTER N ",N
50    PRINT MID$(X$,M,N)
60    PRINT
70 UNTIL M<0
80 END
```

Run the program and experiment with various values of M and N. In particular, you should try values which are outside the bounds of the string, for example

```
M=0    N=4
M=0    N=20
M=8    N=4
M=12   N=0
```

Does the computer behave as you expect?

- -

Type

```
10 DAYS$="//MONTUEWEDTHUFRISATSUN"
20 REPEAT
30    INPUT "ENTER DAY ",DAY
40    IF DAY=0 THEN 80
50    IF DAY>7 THEN 30
60    PRINT MID$(DAYS$, DAY*3, 3)
70    PRINT
80 UNTIL DAY=0
90 END
```

Run the program and enter DAY values of 1, 2,... 7. Does the program work correctly? Study the program carefully, and make sure that you understand how it works.

- -

15.4 An example program

The program in Figure 15.1 plays GUESS-THE-WORD (often called 'Hangman'). The computer chooses a word, and you have to guess it. You do so by selecting letters that you think may be in the word. For each letter that you enter, the computer shows you the position in the word of each occurrence of that letter. Suppose the computer thought of the word ALPHABET.

The computer displays ———————— to start with, showing that there are eight letters in the word.

Suppose your first guess is the letter A. The computer displays A---A--- showing where the A's occur.

If your next guess is the letter T, the computer will display A---A--T. You now know the position of the A's and the T's.

Hence, as you make more guesses, and learn the positions of more letters, the word will become easier to recognise. You are allowed 15 guesses altogether.

```
 10 REM GUESS-THE-WORD   (GUESSWORD1)
 20 DIM SOFAR$(20)
 30
 40 WORD$="ALPHABET"
 50 NUMBER=LEN(WORD$)
 60
 70 FOR K=1 TO NUMBER
 80    SOFAR$(K)="-"
 90 NEXT K
100 FOUND=0
110 USED$=""
120
130 FOR GUESS=1 TO 15
140
150    INPUT "GUESS A LETTER ",GUESS$
160    FOR K=1 TO LEN(USED$)
170      IF GUESS$=MID$(USED$,K,1) THEN 150
180    NEXT K
190    USED$=USED$+GUESS$
200
210    FOR K=1 TO NUMBER
220      IF GUESS$=MID$(WORD$,K,1) THEN
             SOFAR$(K)=GUESS$ :
             FOUND=FOUND+1
230    NEXT K
240
250    FOR K=1 TO NUMBER
260      PRINT SOFAR$(K);
270    NEXT K
280    PRINT "         ";USED$
290    PRINT
300
310    IF FOUND=NUMBER THEN
             PRINT "YOU FOUND THE WORD IN ";GUESS;" GUESSES" :
             END
320
330 NEXT GUESS
340
350 PRINT "YOU HAVE HAD 15 GUESSES"
360 PRINT "THE WORD WAS ";WORD$
370 END
```

Annotations in margin: line 40 "ALPHABET"; line 60 "8"; line 80 "underline"; line 110 "NULL string"

Figure 15.1:   An example program to play GUESS-THE-WORD. As the
                program stands the computer always selects the
                word APLHABET. If you want to change the word you
                will have to modify Line 40. Section 16.2 shows
                how you can store a number of words in memory, and
                get the computer to select one at random.

The following notes describe how the program works:

Line 40   The word selected by the computer is stored in a
                  string variable called WORD$.

Line 50   The length of the word is determined using the LEN
                  function, and stored in a variable called NUMBER.

Line 20   The string array SOFAR$ is used to hold the
                  skeleton of the word as the player has guessed it
                  so far. Using the example just described

                      at the start   SOFAR$ contains --------
                      after Guess 1   SOFAR$ contains A---A---
                      after Guess 2   SOFAR$ contains A---A--T

Lines 70-90   The SOFAR$ array is set to --------. Although
                  there are 20 boxes in the array, we are only using
                  the first eight (as held in NUMBER) because there
                  are only eight letters in the word.

Lines 130, 330 are a FOR loop which allows the player 15 guesses.

Line 150   asks the player to enter his guess. Notice that
                  the computer can tell the difference between GUESS
                  (an ordinary variable) and GUESS$ (a string
                  variable).

Lines 160-190   check that the letter hasn't been entered before.
                  The letters that have been used previously are
                  stored in the string called USED$. The current
                  GUESS$ is compared in turn with each character in
                  USED$. If found in USED$, the letter has been used
                  before, and the player is asked to re-enter his
                  guess. If not found in USED$, the new letter is
                  concatenated to the USED$ string in Line 190.
                  To start with, USED$ is set to the null string by
                  Line 110.

Lines 210-230   check each letter of WORD$ to see if it is the
                  same as the current GUESS$. If it is, the
                  corresponding box of SOFAR$ is set to that letter,
                  and 1 is added to the number of letters found
                  (held in FOUND).

Lines 250-270   display the SOFAR$ array.

Line 280   displays the letters used so far.

Line 310   terminates the program if the player has guessed
                  all the letters.

Lines 350-360   are only executed if the player uses all his
                  fifteen guesses, and doesn't find the word.

- -

Type the program into your computer. Check that you have typed it
correctly. Now run the program. Does it work correctly? If not,
go back and correct it.

- -

When the program is working correctly, save it on your cassette
as GUESSWORD1. Don't forget to fill in the 'cassette contents'
sheet.

- -

15.5 String variables and number variables

- -

Type
```
     A$="3"
     B$="1"
     PRINT A$+B$
```

We can store any character in a string variable, including the
numeric digits 0, 1,.. 9. Here, we store the string "3" in A$,
and the string "1" in B$. When applied to strings, '+' does not
mean 'add' but means 'concatenate'. Hence, A$+B$ results in the
2-character string "31".

- -

Type
```
     PRINT A$-B$
```

The computer will display the error message 'Type mismatch'. '-'
can only be used with numbers or number variables; it cannot be
used with strings, because they are not the right 'type' of
variable. Hence, we have a 'type' mismatch.
     Numbers can be stored in 'string variables'. However, we
cannot perform arithmetic on them – we can only manipulate them
as strings. If we want to perform arithmetic, we must store our
numbers in 'number' variables, for example

```
     A=3 : B=1 : PRINT A+B : PRINT A-B
```

Questions

1. What is a <u>string</u>?

2. How long is the string "XRY 382 T"?

3. What is a <u>null string</u>?

4. What is the maximum string length allowed on the BBC computer?

5. How do you tell the computer that a variable is actually a string variable?

6. What BASIC function do you use to find the length of a string?

7. What is meant by <u>concatenation</u>?

8. Write an assignment command which will concatenate the strings held in Q$ and R$, and store the resulting string in P$.

9. What is a <u>substring</u>?

10* Write an assignment:

    a)   which will store the first four characters of B$ in A$. Use the LEFT$ function.

    b)   Which will store the last four characters of B$ in A$. Use the RIGHT$ function.

    c)   As for a), but use the MID$ function.

    d)   As for b), but use the MID$ function (you will also need to use the LEN function).

11. The BBC computer provides the INSTR (meaning INSTRing) function to search one string for any occurrence of another string. Experiment with this function by writing small throw-away programs, and find out exactly it provides.

12* Line 160 of the GUESS-THE-WORD program is

        FOR K=1 TO LEN(USED$)

Are there any problems when USED$ contains the null string? If so, how can you modify the program?

16 More about input

16.1 READ and DATA commands

Up to now, we have entered data at the keyboard in response to an INPUT command, when the program is being executed. Another way of getting data into a program is to store it in DATA commands within the program itself, and to READ the items of data from these DATA commands. An example will illustrate this.

Type
```
 10 READ A$
 20 PRINT "A$ CONTAINS ";A$
 30 READ B
 40 PRINT "B  CONTAINS ";B
 50 READ C$
 60 PRINT "C$ CONTAINS ";C$
 70 DATA "ALPHA"
 80 DATA 10
 90 DATA "BRAVO"
100 END
```

The items of data contained in the DATA commands are formed into a data list by the computer, in the same order as they appear in the program:

```
     "ALPHA"    10    "BRAVO"
```

Every time the computer comes to a READ command, it takes the next item of data from this data list, and assigns it to the variable specified in the READ command. Run this program, and check that it works correctly (A$ should contain "ALPHA", B should contain 10, and C$ should contain "BRAVO").

- -

Type
```
 70 DATA "ALPHA", 10, "BRAVO"
```

and delete Line 80 and Line 90. Several data items may be placed in a single DATA command, so long as they are separated by commas. Run the program and check that it performs correctly.

- -

Type

```
70 DATA "ALPHA", "BRAVO", 10
```

and run the program. The string "ALPHA" is assigned to A$, but when the computer tries to execute the READ B command in Line 30, it finds that the next item in the data list is the string "BRAVO". A string cannot be assigned to a 'number' memory box, so the computer will tell you that you have made a mistake.

- -

Type

```
70 DATA "ALPHA", 10
```

and run the program. The computer should tell you that you have made a mistake because you haven't provided sufficient data items (two data items for three READ commands).

- -

Type

```
NEW
10 DIM MONTH$(12)
20
30 FOR K=1 TO 12
40    READ MONTH$(K)
50    PRINT MONTH$(K)
60 NEXT K
70
80 DATA "JAN", "FEB", "MAR", "APR", "MAY", "JUN"
90 DATA "JUL", "AUG", "SEP", "OCT", "NOV", "DEC"
100 END
```

and run the program. Does the program perform correctly? If not, go back and correct it. Study the program carefully, and make sure you understand how it works.

```
**********************************************************************
*                                                                    *
*      Any number of DATA commands can be included in a program.     *
*      They can be placed anywhere. It is good practice, however,    *
*      to group them at the end of the program.                      *
*                                                                    *
*      An item in the data list must be the same type (string or     *
*      number) as the variable into which it is being read.          *
*                                                                    *
*      There must be sufficient items in the data list to match      *
*      the number of READ commands executed in the program.          *
*                                                                    *
**********************************************************************
```

DATA commands are normally used when the data required by the program is the same each time the program is run. In the previous example it is unlikely that the names of the months will change!

16.2 Modifying the GUESS-THE-WORD program

The GUESS-THE-WORD program developed in the previous unit always used the same word for you to guess (ALPHABET). It would be an improvement if the program held a number of words, and chose one at random. We can use DATA commands to do this.

```
40 READ WORDS
41 POSITION=RND(WORDS)
42 FOR K=1 TO POSITION
43    READ WORD$
44 NEXT K

361
362 DATA 10
363 DATA "TELEVISION", "KEYBOARD"
364 DATA "COMPUTER", "MEMORY"
365 DATA "VARIABLE", "CASSETTE"
366 DATA "CATALOGUE", "EDITING"
367 DATA "PROGRAMMING", "ANALYSIS"
```

Line 40   reads the first data item (10) and stores it in the variable called WORDS. This tells the computer that there are 10 words in the data list.

Line 41   selects a number at random between 1 and 10. This number is stored in POSITION. Suppose it is 7.

Lines 42-44   make up a FOR loop which repeatedly reads a data item and stores it in the string variable WORD$. When this loop terminates, WORD$ will contain the 7th data item ("CATALOGUE").

- -

Load GUESSWORD1 from your cassette and check that it runs correctly.

- -

Type Lines 40-44 and Lines 361-367 into your program. List it, and check that your typing is correct. Now run the program a number of times, and check that the computer selects a word at random from the list of words within the program.

- -

When the program is working correctly, save it on your cassette as GUESSWORD2.

- -

16.3 The RESTORE command

Type

```
10 READ A$
20 PRINT A$
30 READ B$
40 PRINT B$
50 DATA "JAN", "FEB"
60 END
```

List the program, and check that you have typed it correctly. Now run the program. The output should be:

```
JAN
FEB
```

The computer forms the items of data contained in the DATA command into a data list.

```
"JAN"    "FEB"
```

When the computer executes the READ A$ command, it takes the first data item from the list ("JAN") and stores it in A$. The next available item in the data list is now "FEB". This is read and stored in B$ when the READ B$ command is executed.

- -

Type

```
25 RESTORE
```

and run the program. The output should be:

```
JAN
JAN
```

The READ A$ command is executed as before. The effect of the RESTORE command, however, is to restore the data list to its original state, i.e. "JAN" is the next available data item in the list. Hence, the READ B$ reads and stores "JAN" in B$. The RESTORE command is used when you need to re-read a list of items. This is illustrated in Example Program III (Section 30.5).

16.4   Single character input

At the end of a game, you may wish the computer to ask the player whether or not he wants another game.

Type

```
10 REPEAT
20    INPUT "ANOTHER GAME (Y/N) ",REPLY$
30 UNTIL REPLY$="Y" OR REPLY$="N"
40 PRINT "REPLY IS OK"
50 END
```

and run the program. The ANOTHER GAME question should be asked over and over again, until you enter either Y or N. These are the only acceptable replies. The OR in Line 30 is explained in Unit 18, but its meaning here is obvious.

_ _

Run the program again, and type YES and NO. You should find that both these replies are unaccceptable (to the computer, YES is not the same as Y). We can make these acceptable by using only the first letter of the input.

Type

```
25 ..REPLY$=LEFT$(REPLY$,1)
```

replacing the two dots by two spaces. Now run the program several times, and try entering YES, NO, Y and N. You should find that these replies are now acceptable. In fact, anything beginning with Y or N is accepted.

_ _

The INPUT command waits for you to enter your reply via the keyboard. It is only after you have pressed the RETURN key that the computer acts on your input. Many computers provide a command that causes the computer to wait for you to press ONE key, and then continue when you have done so. You do not need to press the RETURN key. On the BBC computer, this command is GET$.

Type

```
10 REPEAT
20    PRINT "ANOTHER GAME (Y/N) ";
30    REPLY$=GET$
40    PRINT REPLY$
50 UNTIL REPLY$="Y" OR REPLY$="N"
60 PRINT "REPLY IS OK"
70 END
```

List the program, and check that you have typed it correctly. Now run the program. It should perform exactly as before, except that it responds to every character that you type, and does not wait for the RETURN key to be pressed.

Line 30   tells the computer to wait for ONE key to be pressed. This character is stored in REPLY$.

Line 40   The character obtained by the GET$ command is not displayed on the screen (compare this with the INPUT command). Hence, we need the PRINT REPLY$ command to display what has just been typed.

- -

Modify your program to become:

```
10 PRINT "ANOTHER GAME (Y/N) ";
20 REPEAT
30   REPLY$=GET$
40 UNTIL REPLY$="Y" OR REPLY$="N"
50 PRINT REPLY$
60 PRINT "REPLY IS OK"
70 END
```

This is another way of using the GET$ command. Run the program, and see how it performs. The ANOTHER GAME question is asked once. Then follows a repeat loop containing a GET$ command. This loop is repeatedly executed until you enter a Y or an N. Since the GET$ command doesn't echo the character onto the screen, you see nothing displayed until you press Y or N. This program gives the impression that you cannot type any character other than Y or N.

- -

The GET$ command waits for you to press a single key. Many computers provide a command that causes the computer simply to check whether any key has been pressed. The computer then goes on to the next command. It does not wait for a key to be pressed. On the BBC computer, this command is INKEY$.

Type
```
 NEW
10 REPEAT
20   PRINT "PRESS ANY KEY"
30   REPLY$=INKEY$(0)
40 UNTIL REPLY$<>""
50 PRINT "REPLY IS ";REPLY$
60 END
```

List the program, and check that you have typed it correctly. Now run the program. The invitation to PRESS ANY KEY is repeatedly displayed on the screen because of the repeat loop. The INKEY$ command in Line 30 causes the computer to check whether a key has been pressed. If not, REPLY$ is set to the null string (""), otherwise it is set to the character of the key pressed. Run the program several times, and make sure that you understand how it works.

- -

The 0 in INKEY$(0) tells the computer to wait no time before testing whether a key has been pressed, i.e. to test it immediately. If we change this to say 50, then the computer will pause for 50 hundredths of a second (i.e. half a second) before testing whether a key has been pressed.

Type

        30 ..REPLY$=INKEY$(50)

and run the program. Notice how much more slowly the PRESS ANY KEY messages are displayed on the screen. Experiment with different pauses (20, 100, and so on).

- -

```
*****************************************************************
*                                                               *
*      The INPUT command accepts input from the keyboard. The    *
*      computer continues to the next command only after the     *
*      RETURN key has been pressed.                              *
*                                                                *
*      The GET$ command accepts a single character from the      *
*      keyboard. The computer continues to the next command when *
*      ONE key has been pressed. No RETURN key is necessary.     *
*                                                                *
*      The INKEY$ command tests to see whether any key has been  *
*      pressed. If so, then that character is input, otherwise   *
*      a null string is input. You can cause the computer to     *
*      pause for a few hundredths of a second. Then the next     *
*      command is executed - the computer does not wait for you  *
*      to press a key. This command is useful in games such as   *
*      Star-Wars, where the player may control the direction of  *
*      his spaceship by pressing keys. The computer merely tests *
*      to see whether he has pressed a key, rather than waiting  *
*      for him to do so.                                         *
*                                                                *
*****************************************************************
```

16.5 Variations of the READ command

Type

```
10 READ A$, B$
20 PRINT A$
30 PRINT B$
40 DATA "JAN", "FEB"
50 END
```

List the program, and check that you have typed it correctly. Now run the program. Does it perform as you expect? The output should be:

    JAN
    FEB

Several variables can be used in one READ command, just as several variables can be written in one PRINT command. The same applies to the INPUT command. Hence, READ A$, B$ is the same as READ A$ followed by READ B$.

Questions

1.   What new commands have you met in this unit?

2.   From where does the READ command get its data?

3.   What errors can arise with READ and DATA commands?

4.   What is the purpose of the RESTORE command?

5.   What differences are there between the INPUT command, the GET$ command, and the INKEY$ command on the BBC computer?

17 Sorting and searching

17.1 Alphabetical order

Arrange the following children into alphabetical order, and write your answer on a sheet of paper:

```
JOHN    SMITH
SUSAN   DAVISON
ALISON  JONES
JOHN    DAVIS
MARTIN  COATS
DAVID   COATS
ANN     SMART
JAMES   BOOTH
```

Your thinking was probably something like this. Look through the column of Last-Names, and find the name whose first letter is nearest to the beginning of the alphabet. This is BOOTH, because there are no names beginning with A, and no other names beginning with B. Write down JAMES BOOTH on the sheet of paper, and cross it off the list.

Look through the column of Last-Names again, and find the name or names whose first letter is now nearest to the beginning of the alphabet. This is COATS, and there are two occurrences (MARTIN and DAVID). To put these into their correct order, we would need to refer to the First-Names, and write DAVID COATS before MARTIN COATS, because D comes before M in the alphabet. Cross these names off the list.

Now look through the column of Last-Names again, and find the name or names whose first letter is nearest to the beginning of the alphabet. We find DAVISON and DAVIS. The first five letters of DAVISON are the same as DAVIS. However, the shorter name is written first, so DAVIS comes before DAVISON.

This process is repeated for the remaining names. In the case of SMITH and SMART, the first two letters are the same (SM), but the third letter of SMART (A) comes before the third letter of SMITH (I) in the alphabet, and so SMART is written before SMITH.

We can get the computer to arrange a list of names into alphabetical order, just as we have done here.

17.2 Comparing strings

The computer can compare one string with another string, just as it can compare one number with another number.

Type

```
10 REPEAT
20    INPUT "ENTER LAST NAME 1 ",NAME1$
30    INPUT "ENTER LAST NAME 2 ",NAME2$
40
50    IF NAME1$=NAME2$ THEN
         PRINT NAME1$;" IS EQUAL TO ";NAME2$ :
         GOTO 90
60
70    IF NAME1$<NAME2$ THEN
         PRINT NAME1$;" IS LESS THAN ";NAME2$
      ELSE
         PRINT NAME1$;" IS GREATER THAN ";NAME2$
80
90    PRINT
100 UNTIL NAME1$="END"
110 END
```

List the program, and check that you have typed it correctly. Now run the program, and enter the following strings. Write down whether the result is 'less than', 'equal to' or 'greater than'.

NAME1$	NAME2$	<	=	>
BOOTH	COATS	yes		
COATS	BOOTH			
COATS	COATS			
SMITH	SMART			
DAVIS	DAVISON			
BCD	XYZ			
BCD	BCE			
XYZ	BCD			
ABC	ABCD			

NAME1$	NAME2$	<	=	>
1	A			
1	a			
A	a			
a	z			
A	Z			
1	9			

When one string is less than another string, it means that it comes before the other string when arranged in alphabetical order.

17.3 Sorting

Let us now see how we can get the computer to sort a list of names into alphabetical order. There are many methods for sorting on a computer. The method described here is one of the simplest to understand, and is called sorting by selection. If you want to know more about sorting, you should consult a more advanced book (e.g. Basic Statistical Computing, D. Cooke and others, Edward Arnold).

The following commands set up a list of names. In Line 10, we allow for up to 20 names. Line 30 reads the actual size of the list into a variable called SIZE. It is 8 in this example.

```
10 DIM TABLE$(20)
20
30 READ SIZE
40 FOR K=1 TO SIZE
50    READ TABLE$(K)
60    PRINT K;"    ";TABLE$(K)
70 NEXT K
80 PRINT
90

200
210 DATA 8
220 DATA "SMITH", "DAVISON", "JONES", "DAVIS"
230 DATA "COATS", "COATS", "SMART", "BOOTH"
240 END
```

The resulting TABLE$ array is:

SMITH	DAVISON	JONES	DAVIS	COATS	COATS	SMART	BOOTH
1	2	3	4	5	6	7	8

The basis of 'Sorting by Selection' is to select the smallest item from the list, that is, the one whose first letter is nearest to the beginning of the alphabet. This item becomes the first item of the sorted list, and it is then deleted from the list being sorted. Now the smallest of the remaining items is selected, and this becomes the second item of the sorted list. This process is repeated for all the other items in the list, until the whole list has been sorted. The following commands select the smallest item in the array:

```
110 ..SMALLEST$=TABLE$(1)
120 ..POSITION=1
130 ..FOR K=2 TO SIZE
140 ..  IF TABLE$(K)<SMALLEST$ THEN
            SMALLEST$=TABLE$(K) :
            POSITION=K
150 ..NEXT K
```

Line 110   sets SMALLEST$ to the contents of TABLE$(1)

Line 120   records the fact that the smallest item is currently in Box 1

Lines 130–150   make up a FOR loop which compares all the remaining boxes of the array with SMALLEST$. If the contents of a particular box are smaller than SMALLEST$, then SMALLEST$ is set to this value and the new position of the smallest item is stored in POSITION.

The following trace should clarify how this portion of program works. The line-numbers in the left-most column refer to the line-numbers in the program. When Line 110 is executed, then SMALLEST$ is set to the contents of TABLE$(1), which is SMITH in this example. This is shown by writing SMITH in the column headed SMALLEST$. Likewise, Line 120 sets POSITION to 1, so 1 is written in the column headed POSITION. And so on.

Line	SMALLEST$ POSITION	K	TABLE$(K)	condition
110	SMITH			
120	1			
130		2	DAVISON	
140				TRUE: DAVISON is < SMITH
140	DAVISON			
140	2			
130		3	JONES	
140				FALSE: JONES not < DAVISON
130		4	DAVIS	
140				TRUE: DAVIS is < DAVISON
140	DAVIS			
140	4			
130		5	COATS	
140				TRUE: COATS is < DAVIS
140	COATS			
140	5			
130		6	COATS	
140				FALSE: COATS not < COATS
130		7	SMART	
140				FALSE: SMART not < COATS
130		8	BOOTH	
140				TRUE: BOOTH is < COATS
140	BOOTH			
140	8			

At the end of the loop, SMALLEST$ contains BOOTH, and POSITION contains 8. Our next step is to display BOOTH on the screen, and then delete it from the list being sorted.

```
    160
    170 ..PRINT POSITION;"    ";TABLE$(POSITION)
    180 ..TABLE$(POSITION)="ZZZZZZZZ"
```

We use ZZZZZZZZ to indicate that an item has been deleted because all other items in the table will be less than this.

PRACTICAL EXERCISES

Type the program into your computer as it stands at present. List it and check that you have typed it correctly. Now run the program. The output should be:

    8   BOOTH

showing that the program has selected the smallest item.

- -

We now need to repeat the selection of the smallest item in the list, until the whole list has been sorted.
Type
    100 FOR LOOP=1 TO SIZE

    190 NEXT LOOP

Run the program again, and check that the items are printed in alphabetical order. Notice that when two items are the same (COATS in this example), the one which was first in the original list is printed first (COATS in Position 5 comes before COATS in Position 6). To put these two items into their correct order, you would now have to refer to their First-names.
    Save the program on your cassette as NAMESORT1.

- -

17.4 Searching

In Unit 15 we saw how the names of the twelve months can be held in the computer, using an array of strings. This is often called a table.

MONTH$	JAN	FEB	MAR	APR	MAY	JUN	JUL	AUG	SEP	OCT	NOV	DEC
	1	2	3	4	5	6	7	8	9	10	11	12

The process of finding a particular item in a table is called searching. Suppose we have a date in the form 15NOV84, and we want to convert it to the form 15/11/84, where 11 means the eleventh month. How do we convert the text form of the month (NOV) to its numeric form (11)? The simplest way is to carry out a linear search of the table. Since all the months are stored in the MONTH$ array, we can start at the beginning of the array, and compare NOV with each box in turn.

Compare NOV with Box 1 (JAN) : does not match.
Compare NOV with Box 2 (FEB) : does not match.
.....
Compare NOV with Box 10 (OCT) : does not match.
Compare NOV with Box 11 (NOV) : match.

When a match is found, the position of the box tells us the numeric form of the date.

PRACTICAL EXERCISES

- -

Type

```
10 DIM MONTH$(12)
20
30 FOR K=1 TO 12
40    READ MONTH$(K)
50 NEXT K
60
70 REPEAT
80    PRINT
90    INPUT "ENTER MONTH ",REPLY$
100   REPLY$=LEFT$(REPLY$,3)
110   IF REPLY$="END" THEN 170
120
130   FOR K=1 TO 12
140     IF MONTH$(K)=REPLY$ THEN
          PRINT REPLY$;" IS MONTH ";K :
          GOTO 170
150   NEXT K
160   PRINT REPLY$;" IS NOT A MONTH"
170 UNTIL REPLY$="END"
180
190 DATA "JAN", "FEB", "MAR", "APR", "MAY", "JUN"
200 DATA "JUL", "AUG", "SEP", "OCT", "NOV", "DEC"
210 END
```

List the program, and check that you have typed it correctly. Now run the program with the following data:

JAN   MAR   JUN   DEC   FEBRUARY   ABCDE   END

Does the program produce the correct output? The following notes may help you understand how the program works:

Line 90   asks the user to enter the name of the month.

Line 100   accepts only the first three letters of those
                   typed. Hence, FEBRUARY becomes FEB. Remember that
                   only the first three letters of each month are
                   stored in the table itself.

Lines 130-150   make up a FOR loop which compares each element of
                   the MONTH$ array with REPLY$. If a match is found,
                   then the numeric month is displayed by Line 140.
                   If no match is found, then Line 160 is executed,
                   after the loop has been executed twelve times.

- -

Run the program again, and test it by entering all twelve months
(JAN, FEB,... DEC). The program will stop with the error:

    TOO MANY FORs

This occurs because when a match is found the FOR loop is left at
Line 140 without executing a NEXT command, and if you do this
more than ten times on the BBC computer, an error occurs. To
overcome this problem, modify Lines 140 and 160 to become:

    140 ..IF MONTH$(K)=REPLY$ THEN
           PRINT REPLY$;" IS MONTH ";K :
           K=1000

    160 ..IF K=13 THEN PRINT REPLY$;" IS NOT A MONTH"

replacing the two dots by two spaces. Run the program again, and
test it by entering all twelve months. The previous error should
now have disappeared. In Line 140, if MONTH$(K) is equal to
REPLY$ then the month is displayed on the screen, and K is set to
some arbitrarily high value (1000 here) so as to terminate the
loop. If no match is found at all, the loop will be executed
twelve times, and will terminate with K having a value of 13. In
this case, Line 160 will be executed to explain that the string
in REPLY$ is not a valid month. This example illustrates the
problems that can be encountered on the BBC computer when jumping
out of FOR loops.

- -

17.5 ASCII representations

How does the computer know how to put characters into their
correct order? Simple. A computer stores all characters in its
memory as number codes. A common set of number codes used by a
lot of computers is called the American Standard Code for
Information Interchange, or ASCII for short.

- -

Type

```
10 FOR K=1 TO 6
20    READ X$
30    PRINT X$;"   ASCII = ";ASC(X$)
40 NEXT K
50
60 DATA "0", "9", "A", "Z", "a", "z"
70 END
```

List the program, and check that you have typed it correctly. Now
run the program. The output should be:

```
0  ASCII = 48
9  ASCII = 57
A  ASCII = 65
Z  ASCII = 90
a  ASCII = 97
z  ASCII = 122
```

The letter A is stored within the computer as the number code 65,
and the letter Z is stored as the number code 90. When the
computer compares characters, it really compares their number
codes. Since 65 is less than 90, the letter A comes before the
letter Z. Likewise 'a' (number code 97) comes before 'z' (number
code 122). In particular notice that:

the numbers 0..9 come before the capital letters A..Z;
the numbers 0..9 come before the small letters a..z;
the capital letters A..Z come before the small letters a..z.

Check that this agrees with the results you obtained from the
experiment you carried out in Section 17.2. The function ASC(X$)
in Line 30 converts the first character of the string between the
brackets - X$ in this example - into its ASCII number code.
Hence, in this way, you can find out the ASCII number code for
any character.

- -

Type

```
NEW
10 FOR K=32 TO 126
20    PRINT K;"    ";CHR$(K)
30    X$=INKEY$(100)
40 NEXT K
50 END
```

List the program, and check that you have typed it correctly. Now run the program. The output on the screen should give you the character corresponding to the ASCII number codes from 32 to 126. ASCII codes actually extend from 0 to 127, but the codes between 0 and 31, and code 127, are special control codes which have peculiar effects on the screen, so it is best not to try to display them. The function CHR$(K) in Line 20 converts the ASCII number code stored in K into the character that it represents. Hence, CHR$ has the opposite effect to ASC. Line 30 is a delay that makes the output easier to read on the screen.

- -

In Section 10.4 we used CHR$(7). 7 is an ASCII number code whose effect is to ring the bell.

Type

```
PRINT CHR$(7)
```

and confirm that the bell does indeed ring.

- -

Questions

1.   What new commands have you met in this unit?

2.   What does ASCII stand for?

3.   How does the computer know the order into which to sort characters?

4.   What is the purpose of the function ASC(X$)?

5.   What is the purpose of the function CHR$(K)?

6.   What is <u>sorting by selection</u>?

7.   What is a <u>table</u>?

8.   Explain what is meant by <u>searching</u>.

9.   What is a <u>linear search</u>?

10*   Write a program which uses 'sorting by selection' to sort the following numbers into ascending order:

        21   17   3   97   84   27   11   9   21

Hint: this program is very similar to the one described in Section 17.3 (saved on your cassette as NAMESORT1), but with a 'number' array rather than a 'string' array.

11*   Write a program which accepts a string of capital and small letters as input, and prints the string in capitals, that is, all small letters are converted to capitals.

        Input: This is a VERY SILLY exercise
        Output: THIS IS A VERY SILLY EXERCISE

Hint: Capital letters have ASCII codes in the range 65..90. Small letters have ASCII codes in the range 97..122.

           Any character with an ASCII code in the range 97..122 (a small letter) should have 32 subtracted from its ASCII code, to convert it into a capital letter.

18 Grouped conditions

You often need to test for more than one condition at a time.

Type

```
10 FOR K=1 TO 8
20    PRINT K;
30    IF K<3 OR K>6 THEN PRINT " IS OK";
40    PRINT
50 NEXT K
60 END
```

List the program, and check that you have typed it correctly. Now run the program. The output should be:

```
1 IS OK
2 IS OK
3
4
5
6
7 IS OK
8 IS OK
```

We have two conditions in Line 30 (K<3 and K>6) joined together by the word OR. The message 'IS OK' is printed alongside a number if:

    <u>either</u> the number is less than 3
    <u>or</u>   the number is greater than 6.

- -

Modify Line 30 to become:

```
30 ..IF K>3 AND K<6 THEN PRINT " IS OK";
```

and run the program. This time we have two conditions (K>3 and K<6) joined together by the word AND. The message 'IS OK' is printed alongside a number if:

    <u>both</u> the number is greater than 3
    <u>and</u> the number is less than 6.

The only numbers that satisfy these combined conditions are 4 and 5. The number 6, for example, is greater than 3, but it is not less than 6, so it is ruled out.

- -

Modify Line 30 to become:

```
30 ..IF NOT (K>3 AND K<6) THEN PRINT " IS OK";
```

and run the program. As in English, the word NOT negates the condition. Hence, only those numbers which do not satisfy the combined conditions are acceptable in this case. These are 1, 2, 3, 6, 7 and 8. The condition NOT (K>3 AND K<6) is the same as the condition (K<=3 OR K>=6). Try it and see.

- -

Type
```
10 REPEAT
20    INPUT "ENTER YOUR CHOICE (0-6) ",REPLY$
30    REPLY$=LEFT$(REPLY$,1)
40 UNTIL REPLY$>="0" AND REPLY$<="6"
50 END
```

and run the program several times, testing it with a variety of inputs. You should find that only 0, 1, 2, 3, 4, 5 and 6 are acceptable, and every other character is invalid. This fragment of code illustrates that combined conditions can also appear in the UNTIL clause of a REPEAT loop.

- -

Question

1*   Work out which numbers will have the message 'IS OK' printed alongside if you change Line 30 of the first program in this unit to:

a)   30 ..IF K<=4 OR K>5 THEN PRINT " IS OK";

b)   30 ..IF K>0 AND K>4 THEN PRINT " IS OK";

c)   30 ..IF NOT(K<=2 OR K>7) THEN PRINT " IS OK";

d)   30 ..IF K<2 AND K>6 THEN PRINT " IS OK";

19 More about output

19.1 Zones

The PRINT command is used in almost every program you write. You may recall that we have studied the PRINT command already – in Section 4.1. In this unit, we will be looking at some further features of the PRINT command.

In BASIC, the screen of your computer behaves as if it is divided into vertical zones. The width of a zone varies from one version of BASIC to another, as do the number of zones across the screen. For example, a 40-character screen may have 4 zones, each 10 characters wide, as shown below:

```
ZONE        1              2              3              4
      ┌──────────────┬──────────────┬──────────────┬──────────────┐
      │1          10 │11         20 │21         30 │31         40 │
      │              │              │              │              │
      │              │              │              │              │
      └──────────────┴──────────────┴──────────────┴──────────────┘
```

SCREEN

This is the standard form of the screen on the BBC computer, and we will assume this form for the remainder of the unit.

19.2 Commas and semicolons in print lists

Type
```
10 PRINT "123456789*123456789*123456789*123456789*"
20 PRINT "A", "B", "C", "D"
30 END
```

and run the program. The numbers displayed on the screen by Line 10 are to help you pick out the zones and the character columns across the screen. There are asterisks at character columns 10, 20, 30, and 40. Notice that each item in the print list begins in a new zone: A goes into the first column of Zone 1, B goes into the first column of Zone 2, and so on. A <u>comma</u> after an item in the print list of a PRINT command causes enough spaces to be printed to ensure that the next item in the print list is output in the next zone.

- -

Type

    20 PRINT "ALPHA", "BETA", "GAMMA", "DELTA"

and run the program. Notice that each item begins in the left-most column of a zone.

- -

Type

    20 PRINT "ALPHABETICALLY", "BETA", "GAMMA", "DELTA"

and run the program. ALPHABETICALLY is too large for Zone 1, so it overflows into Zone 2. BETA now goes into Zone 3, and GAMMA into Zone 4. Since there is no room left on this line, DELTA goes into Zone 1 of the next line.

- -

Type

    20 PRINT "A"; "B"; "C"; "D"

and run the program. A semicolon after an item in the print list causes the next item to be printed on the same line, and immediately following the previous item. The zones are ignored.

- -

Type

    20 PRINT "ALPHABETICALLY"; "BETA"; "GAMMA"; "DELTA"

and run the program. The zones are again ignored.

- -

Type

    20 PRINT 1, 2, 3, 4

and run the program. Notice that each item in the print list is displayed in a new zone, but in the case of numbers, they appear at the right-hand end of the zone. Contrast this with strings which start at the left-hand end of the zone.

- -

Type

    20 PRINT 1, 202, 34567, 87654321

and run the program. Each number is displayed in a new zone, in such a way that its right-most digit appears in the right-most column of the zone.

- -

Type

        20 PRINT 1; 202; 34567; 87654321

and run the program. As with strings, a semicolon after an item
in the print list causes the next item to be printed immediately
following the previous item. The zones are ignored.

- -

In the previous example, the 1 is displayed at the right-hand end
of the first zone. Then the other three items are displayed
immediately following it. If you want the first number to start
in the first column, you can precede it by a semicolon.

Type

        20 PRINT ; 1; 202; 34567; 87654321

and run the program.

- -

This form of output is obviously not clear, as you cannot
distinguish the four numbers.

Type

        20 PRINT ; 1; " "; 202; " "; 34567; " "; 87654321

and run the program. The four numbers should be separated by
spaces, thus making them clearly visible.

- -

```
****************************************************************
*                                                              *
*      Commas are used in PRINT commands when you want to align *
*      the output in vertical columns using the zones. They are *
*      especially useful for aligning numbers.                  *
*                                                              *
*      Semicolons are used in PRINT commands when you want to   *
*      ignore the zones, and space the output yourself.         *
*                                                              *
****************************************************************
```

19.3 The TAB command

The TAB command is useful when you want to specify the precise column at which the next item is to be printed.

Type

```
10 PRINT "123456789*123456789*123456789*123456789*"
20 PRINT TAB(7); "A"; TAB(21); "B"
30 END
```

and run the program. The output should be:

```
123456789*123456789*123456789*123456789*
      A             B
```

Numbering the character positions from 1 to 40 as we have done here, the simplest way to understand the TAB command is to think that TAB(7) prints spaces from the current cursor position up to and including Column 7. Hence, the next item (A in this example) will appear in Column 8. Likewise, TAB(21) will print spaces from the current cursor position up to and including Column 21. Hence, the B will appear in Column 22.

- -

Type

```
10 PRINT "123456789*123456789*123456789*123456789*"
20 FOR K=1 TO 5
30    PRINT TAB(K); K
40 NEXT K
50 END
```

and run the program. A variable can be used with the TAB command, for example, the K in TAB(K).

- -

19.4 Formatted output

Most versions of BASIC provide further facilities to allow you to control the spacing of your output. A special extension of the PRINT command, called PRINT USING, is often used. The BBC computer uses a special variable called @%. However, it is beyond the scope of this book to explain how the @% variable is used.

Questions

1.   What is the effect of a <u>comma</u> in the print list of a PRINT command?

2.   What is the effect of a <u>semicolon</u> in the print list of a PRINT command?

3.   Study the following program, and decide what output will be produced.

```
10 PRINT "123456789*123456789*123456789*123456789*"
20 PRINT 1; "ST", 2; "ND"
30 PRINT ; 3; "RD"; 4; "TH"
40 PRINT 5, "TH", 678; 9
50 PRINT TAB(5); "X"; TAB(38); "Y"
60 END
```

Write down your answers in this grid, then check your answers on your computer.

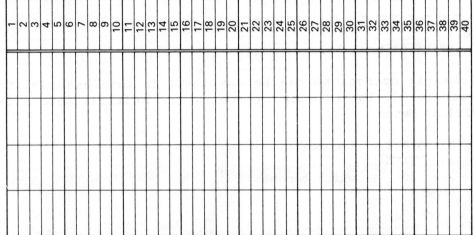

4.   Run the following program, and notice the difference between aligning numbers using zones, and aligning numbers using TAB:

```
10 PRINT "123456789*123456789*123456789*123456789*"
20 PRINT 1
30 PRINT 123
40 PRINT TAB(9); 1
50 PRINT TAB(9); 123
60 END
```

20 Numbers

20.1 Simple arithmetic

In Unit 1 we saw that the computer can perform simple arithmetic
- adding, subtracting, multiplying and dividing.

Type

        PRINT 2+3
        PRINT 5-2
        PRINT 4*5
        PRINT 20/4

and check that each answer is correct.

- -

Type

        PRINT 3+5*2

Arithmetic operations can be combined. In this example, the
answer is 13. The computer performs the multiply before the
addition. Hence

        3 + 5 * 2   becomes

        3 +   10   which becomes

           13

- -

Type

        PRINT (3+5)*2

The answer is 16. By putting brackets around 3+5, we tell the
computer to work this out first, giving an answer of 8. This 8 is
then multiplied by the 2 to give an answer of 16

        (3 + 5) * 2   becomes

           8   * 2   which becomes

              16

- -

Type

      PRINT 8+20/2

The answer is 18. The computer performs the division before the
addition (20/2 = 10, then 8+10 = 18).

- -


```
***********************************************************
*                                                         *
*  BASIC performs arithmetic in a certain priority order: *
*                                                         *
*  1. It works out whatever is contained in brackets. If there *
*     are brackets within brackets, it will do the innermost    *
*     first. For example:                                 *
*                                                         *
*       2 * (3 + (7 - 3) * 2)      becomes                 *
*                                                         *
*       2 * (3 +   4    * 2)       which becomes           *
*                                                         *
*       2 * (3 +        8)         which becomes           *
*                                                         *
*       2 *          11            which becomes           *
*                                                         *
*              22                                         *
*                                                         *
*  2. It works out multiplication and division.          *
*                                                         *
*  3. It works out addition and subtraction.             *
*                                                         *
***********************************************************
```

Type

      PRINT 3+5*2

Multiplication is 2nd in the priority order, whereas addition is
3rd, so the multiplication is done before the addition.

- -

Type

      PRINT 9-4+2

The answer should be 7. Both addition and subtraction are 3rd in
the priority order. When operations of the same priority occur in
the same line, as here, the computer deals with them from left to
right. Hence,

```
9 - 4 + 2        becomes

  5   + 2        which becomes

    7
```

20.2 Decimal numbers

Up to now, we have only used whole numbers in our programs. The computer can also hold decimal numbers (i.e. numbers with a decimal point and a fractional part).

Type
```
PRINT 4/2
PRINT 5/2
PRINT 5/4
PRINT 5/3
```

The first answer is a whole number. All the other answers are decimal numbers.

Type
```
X=4/2
PRINT X
X=14/3
PRINT X
```

A 'number' box in the computer's memory can hold both whole numbers and decimal numbers.

Sometimes we want to convert a decimal number to a whole number, by omitting the decimal part of the number. We can do this with the INT function.

Type
```
X=14/3
PRINT X;"    ";INT(X)
```

The INT function omits the decimal part, leaving the whole number. This process is called truncating the number.

20.3 DIV and MOD

Type

        PRINT 12345/100

The answer should be 123.45, which has both a whole-number part
and a decimal part.

Type

        PRINT 12345 DIV 100

DIV performs a divide just as '/' does, but the answer that it
produces is a whole-number. In this example the answer is 123,
because 12345 divided by 100 goes 123 times, with a remainder of
45. This remainder can be calculated on the computer using MOD.

Type

        PRINT 12345 MOD 100

The answer is 45, the remainder after dividing 12345 by 100.

- -

You may recall that in Unit 12 we used the following expression
to determine the 'team' to which a cross-country runner belonged:

        TEAM=1 + (RUNNER-1) DIV 5

We are now in a position to see how this works.

Type

        10 FOR RUNNER=1 TO 15
        20   PRINT RUNNER, (RUNNER-1), (RUNNER-1) DIV 5
        30 NEXT RUNNER
        40 END

and run the program. In the output:

    Column 1 gives the number of the runner (from 1-15).

    Column 2 gives (RUNNER-1), which varies from 0-14.

    Column 3 shows the result of (Column 2) DIV 5.

            The first five runners have values 0.
            The next five runners have values 1.
            The last five runners have values 2.

    These are converted into the team number by adding 1.

20.4 An example program

A Bank will pay you for saving your money with them. What they pay is called <u>interest</u>, and the amount of the interest depends on the amount you are saving. An <u>interest rate</u> of 10% means the Bank will each year pay you 10 hundredths (one tenth) of the amount you are saving. If you leave the interest at the Bank as well, then it also will attract interest in the following year. This is known as <u>compound interest</u>.

Type

```
 10 REM   INTEREST CALCULATION  (INTEREST1)
 20
 30 RATE=10
 40 INPUT "ENTER AMOUNT ",AMOUNT
 50 INPUT "NUMBER OF YEARS ",YEARS
 60
 70 FOR K=1 TO YEARS
 80    interest = AMOUNT*RATE/100
 90    AMOUNT=AMOUNT+interest
100 NEXT K
110
120 PRINT
130 PRINT "NEW AMOUNT = ";AMOUNT
140 END
```

List the program, and check that you have typed it correctly. Notice that 'interest' is written in small letters, because the first three letters of INTEREST form the reserved word INT. Now run the program for an amount of 10.00, and 6 years. The answer should be something like 17.71561. The following notes may help you to understand the program:

```
Line 30    : The interest rate is 10%.
Line 80    : Calculates interest due each year.
Line 90    : Adds the interest to the amount.
Lines 70-100: Repeat the calculations for a number of years.
```

- -

Notice that the new amount has several decimal digits. Normally, when you are dealing with money, there will be only two decimal digits, representing the number of pence.

Type

```
111 AMOUNTINPENCE=AMOUNT*100
112 POUNDS=AMOUNTINPENCE DIV 100
113 PENCE=AMOUNTINPENCE MOD 100
130 PRINT "NEW AMOUNT = ";POUNDS;" POUNDS   ";PENCE;" PENCE"
```

and rerun the program. The amount should now have two decimal digits. Can you work out how this is done?

- -

Save the program on your cassette as INTEREST1. Don't forget the 'cassette contents' sheet.

- -

Questions

What answers do you think the computer will produce when it executes the following commands? Write down your answers below.

	Your answer	computer
1.	PRINT 3+3*3	
2.	PRINT 9-6/3	
3.	PRINT 7-4+2	
4.	PRINT 3*4/2	
5.	PRINT 9-3*2+1	
6.	PRINT 9-(3*2)+1	
7.	PRINT (9-3)*(2+1)	
8.	PRINT 9/4	
9.	PRINT INT(9/4)	
10.	PRINT 9 DIV 4	
11.	PRINT 9 MOD 4	
12.	PRINT 2*3-4/(5 MOD 2)+1	

Now type the commands into the computer and check whether you were correct.

21 Standard functions

21.1 What is a function?

We have used the word 'function' on several occasions in the previous units, without actually saying what it means. A function carries out a specific task which produces a result. The result may be a 'string' or a 'number', and can be used in a program in exactly the same way as an ordinary string or number. The following examples illustrate what is meant by 'task' and 'result':

Function: MID$("ABCDE",3,2)
Task   : to extract a substring from the string "ABCDE". The substring starts at the 3rd character of the string, and is 2 characters long.
Result : the substring, in this case "CD".

Function: LEN("ABCDE")
Task   : to find the length of the string "ABCDE".
Result : the length of the string, in this case 5.

Function: RND(6)
Task   : to generate a random number in the range 1-6.
Result : the random number.

The following are examples of how functions might be used:

    PRINT MID$("ABCDE",3,2)
    X$=MID$("ABCDE",3,2)

    FOR K=1 TO LEN(X$)

    NUMBER=RND(100)

These examples show that functions have the form:

    function-name(parameters)

The function-name specifies which function is to be used. The items within the brackets are called parameters; these are the actual values that you are asking the function to work on. For example:

RND(100)   tells the RND function to generate a random number between 1 and 100. Here, the parameter is 100.

RND(6)   tells the RND function to generate a random number between 1 and 6. Here, the parameter is 6.

Hence, you can control the precise action of the function by varying the value of the parameter.

21.2 The functions provided with BBC BASIC

BASIC has a number of built-in functions; these are often called the standard functions. They can be divided into three categories:

string functions   such as we have seen in Unit 15, which are concerned with strings:

LEFT$ RIGHT$ MID$ LEN

number functions   such as we have seen in Unit 9 and Unit 20, which are concerned with numbers:

RND INT MOD DIV

In addition, there are several functions which are more mathematical. If you are familiar with mathematics, you will probably understand how these functions are used.

SIN COS TAN DEG RAD PI
ASN ACS ATN
EXP LN   LOG
ABS SGN SQR

These functions are explained in Appendix B.

conversion   which convert 'strings' to 'numbers' and
functions   'numbers' to 'strings'.

ASC CHR$ VAL STR$

Some of these functions have been used earlier. Others have not. A complete explanation of each of these functions can be found in Appendix B.

21.3 User-defined functions

In addition to its standard functions, BASIC allows you to define your own functions. These are explained in Unit 26.

Questions

1.   Explain what is meant by the word <u>function</u>.

2.   What is a <u>parameter</u>?

3.   How many parameters are there in LEFT$("XYZ",2)? What are they?

22 Timing

22.1 Using the computer's clock

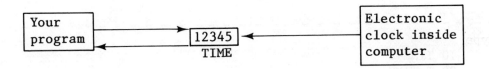

There is an electronic clock inside the BBC computer which your programs can use for timimg. Every one-hundredth of a second, this clock will add 1 to a variable called TIME, and it continues to do so no matter what your program is doing. Hence, the TIME variable can be used to keep track of how much time has passed since some particular event occurred.

- -

Type

```
PRINT TIME
```

The number displayed on the screen shows the amount of time (in hundredths of a second) that has passed since the computer was first switched on.

- -

Type

```
T=TIME
```

The variable T now holds the value that was in TIME when this command was executed. This is the amount of time that has passed since the computer was first switched on.

Type

```
PRINT T
```

This amount of time is displayed on the screen, in hundredths of a second.

Type

```
PRINT T DIV 100, T MOD 100
```

The amount of time is now displayed in seconds and hundredths of a second.

Type

        PRINT TIME DIV 100, TIME MOD 100

Notice that the TIME variable has been increased by the electronic clock while you have been doing these exercises. The difference between T and TIME is the time that it has taken you to do the exercises.

- -

Type

        10 TIME=0
        20 T=TIME
        30 PRINT T DIV 100, T MOD 100
        40 GOTO 20
        50 END

and run the program. The value of the TIME variable (in seconds and hundredths of a second) is repeatedly displayed on the screen. Let the program run for 20-30 seconds, and then press the ESCAPE key. Study the program, and try to understand how it works. Notice that you can give a value to the TIME variable: we set it to zero in Line 10.
    Now look carefully at the output displayed on the screen, and notice that the second number (the hundredths) increases in steps of 2 (and occasionally 3). Why does it not increase in steps of 1, since the electronic clock adds 1 to TIME every one-hundredth of a second? The answer is that our program takes more than two hundredths of a second to execute Lines 30 and 40. Hence, when the computer gets back to Line 20, and samples the value in TIME again, it has increased by two or three hundredths of a second.

- -

If you have a stop-watch, then try the following experiment to see how accurate the clock within the computer is.

    1.   Type RUN but do not press the RETURN key.
    2.   Press the RETURN key, and, <u>at the same time</u>, start your
         watch.
    3.   Do not look at the screen, but keep a careful eye on
         your watch. When it gets to 50 seconds, press the
         ESCAPE key.
    4.   Look at the last time displayed on the screen, and see
         how close it is to 50 seconds.

- -

Type

```
10 DELAY=200
20 TIME=0
30 NOW=TIME
40 REPEAT UNTIL TIME>=NOW+DELAY
50 PRINT TIME
60 END
```

This program causes the computer to pause for a specified length
of time.

Line 10   sets the delay to 200 hundredths of a second, that is,
            2 seconds.

Line 30   sets the variable NOW to the current value in TIME.

Line 40   causes the computer to wait until 2 seconds have
            passed. Notice that there are no commands in the REPEAT
            loop.

Run the program. The program should pause for two seconds before
printing the current value in TIME. You will find that the value
is actually 201, the extra one-hundredth of a second being used
to execute the PRINT command itself.

- -

Type

```
10 DELAY=500
```

and run the program. Does it perform correctly?

- -

Type

```
10 FOR DELAY=1000 TO 6000 STEP 1000
20    TIME=0
30    FOR K=1 TO DELAY : NEXT
40    PRINT TIME,DELAY
50 NEXT DELAY
60 END
```

and run the program. You can use a FOR loop to get the computer
to pause for a period of time, as we have done in Line 30. The
length of the pause can be varied by changing the final value in
the FOR loop. The output should show that a value of 1000 in the
delay loop causes a delay of approximately half a second. If you
wanted a delay of, say, 2 seconds, you would need a value of 4000
in the delay loop.

22.2 Reaction-time program

This program uses the TIME variable to measure the time that it takes a person to react to some event.

- -

Type

```
10 REM   REACTION TESTER   (REACTION1)
20
30 CLS
40 ADDUP=0
50
60 FOR K=1 TO 10
70    DELAY=200+RND(500)
80    NOW=TIME
90    REPEAT UNTIL TIME>NOW+DELAY
100   PRINT CHR$(7);
110
120   TIME=0
130   X$=GET$
140   T=TIME
150
160   ADDUP=ADDUP+T
170   PRINT T
180 NEXT K
190 PRINT
200 PRINT "AVERAGE = ";ADDUP/10;" HUNDREDTHS"
210 END
```

List the program, and check that you have typed it correctly. Now run the program, and make a note of your average reaction time. The following notes may help you to understand how this program works.

Line 30	clears the screen.
Lines 70-90	cause the computer to pause. The length of the pause is random between 200 and 700 hundredths of a second (i.e. between 2 and 7 seconds).
Line 100	sounds the bell. As soon as you hear the bell, press the RETURN key as quickly as you can.
Lines 120-140	measure how long it takes you to press the key. This time is displayed by Line 170.

- -

Type

```
100 ..PRINT "PRESS";
```

Instead of the bell being sounded, the word PRESS is displayed on
the screen. As soon as you see the word on the screen, then press
the RETURN key as quickly as you can. Run the program, and make a
note of your average reaction time. You will probably find that
this average is larger than the previous average – indicating
that you react more quickly to signals from your ears than you do
to signals from your eyes.

- -

Save the program on your cassette as REACTION1. Don't forget to
fill in the 'cassette contents' sheet.

- -

22.3 A digital clock

The following program works as a digital clock. Type it into your
computer.

```
 10 REM   DIGITAL CLOCK   (CLOCK1)
 20
 30 CLS
 40 MAXTIME=24*60*60*100
 50
 60 INPUT "HOURS = ",HOURS
 70 INPUT "MINS  = ",MINS
 80 INPUT "SECS  = ",SECS
 90 TIME=((HOURS*60+MINS)*60+SECS)*100
100
110 REPEAT
120    REPEAT UNTIL (TIME MOD 100)=0
130    IF TIME>=MAXTIME THEN TIME=0
140
150    T=TIME DIV 100
160    SECS =T MOD 60
170    MINS =(T DIV 60) MOD 60
180    HOURS=(T DIV 60) DIV 60
190    PRINT TAB(0,10),HOURS,MINS,SECS
200 UNTIL FALSE
210 END
```

Check that your typing is correct. Now run the program, and set
the clock to

    23 hours   58 mins   30 secs

Check that the clock is working correctly. Press ESCAPE to terminate the program. Run the program again, and try a different starting time.

Study the 'digital clock' program carefully, and try to understand how it works. The following notes may help you.

Lines 60-90   set the clock to some starting value.

Lines 110-200   form a never-ending loop. Since a REPEAT loop continues until the condition is TRUE, and since FALSE can never be TRUE, the loop never ends. You will have to press the ESCAPE key to end the program.

Line 190   TAB(0,10) causes the output to be displayed at one point on the screen. The TAB function is explained in Section 23.4.

- -

Save the program on your cassette as CLOCK1. Don't forget to fill in the 'cassette contents' sheet.

- -

Questions

1.   What does the electronic clock inside your computer do?

2.   What will the command 'PRINT TIME' display on the screen?

3.   What will the command 'LET TIME=0' do?

4.   What command should you use to display the time in seconds and hundredths of a second?

5.   How can you test the accuracy of the electronic clock?

6.   In the Reaction Tester, did you respond more quickly to your ears or to your eyes?

23 Graphics and colour

23.1 Introduction

Many of the computers now cheaply available in shops are able to draw pictures on their screens. These pictures often involve several colours. The ability to draw pictures is called graphics. The BBC computer provides very many facilities for graphics, but it is beyond the scope of this book to deal with them all in detail. Indeed, whole books have been written just on graphics. The aim of this unit, therefore, is to provide you with a basic understanding of graphics, from which you can build a deeper knowledge.

Firstly, we should distinguish between 'text' and 'graphics'.

Text   : Up to now, we have displayed only characters on the screen. These characters have been the same as those which appear on the keyboard. Characters such as these, appearing on the screen, are called text.

Graphics: There are special BASIC commands which instruct the computer to draw lines and shapes on the screen, in a variety of colours. These lines and shapes are referred to as graphics.

The BBC computer has EIGHT modes in which it can operate. These modes are numbered from 0 to 7, and are called Mode 0, Mode 1,... Mode 7. Only one mode can be used at a time. Each mode has different capabilities regarding 'text' and 'graphics'.

The number of characters that can be displayed as text on the screen varies from mode to mode. In Mode 7, for example, there are 25 lines on the screen, and each line can hold 40 characters, making a total of 25x40=1000 characters. In contrast, Mode 0 supports 32 lines, each with 80 characters, giving a total of 2560 characters. The 'text' capabilities of the various modes are summarised in the following table.

Mode	0	1	2	3	4	5	6	7
TEXT								
characters per line	80	40	20	80	40	20	40	40
lines per screen	32	32	32	25	32	32	25	25
GRAPHICS								
pixels horizontally	640	320	160	–	320	160	–	–
pixels vertically	256	256	256	–	256	256	–	–
COLOURS	2	4	16	2	2	4	2	8
MEMORY REQUIRED	20K	20K	20K	16K	10K	10K	8K	1K
AVAILABLE ON MODEL	B	B	B	B	AB	AB	AB	AB

The graphics capability also varies from mode to mode. The quality of the graphics is determined by the number of pixels provided on the screen (the term 'pixel' is explained later). Mode 5 provides 160x256=40960 pixels in total, whereas Mode 0 provides 640x256=163840 pixels in total. Therefore, the graphics provided in Mode 0 is a better quality than, for example, that provided by Mode 5. Notice that Mode 3, Mode 6 and Mode 7 do not support graphics.

The number of colours varies from mode to mode. Mode 2, for example, provides eight colours and eight flashing colours, whereas Mode 5 allows only four colours.

Some of the computer's memory is used for the graphics, and so is not available for your programs. In general, the higher the number of pixels, the greater is the graphics demand for memory. Memory is measured in units of 1K. 1K is approximately one thousand memory boxes, so 16K is approximately 16 thousand memory boxes. Mode 7 needs only 1K of memory, whereas Mode 2, for example, needs 20K of memory. The Model A BBC computer is fitted with 16K of memory, and the Model B comes with 32K. Because Modes 0, 1, 2, and 3 all require 16K or more, these modes are only available on the Model B. Modes 4, 5, 6, and 7 are available on both Model A and Model B.

23.2 Drawing lines

You can think of a computer display screen as consisting of a large number of dots. Each dot can be made to emit light. Hence, by carefully choosing which dots to light up, you can draw pictures on the screen.

BBC BASIC caters for 1280 dots across the screen, and 1024 dots up the screen. The horizontal dots are numbered 0, 1,..1279, and the vertical dots are numbered 0, 1,.. 1023. Numbering starts from the bottom left-hand corner of the screen, as shown in the following diagram:

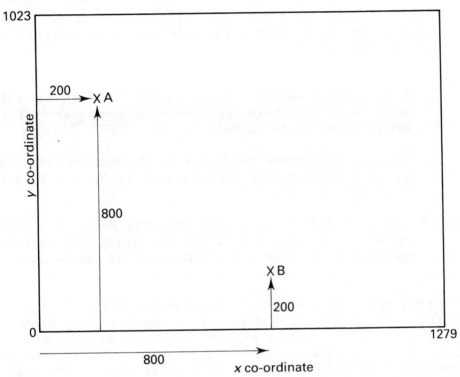

The position of a particular dot on the screen is specified in terms of:

1. how far across the screen the dot is. For example, Dot A is at position 200 across the screen. This is often called the X co-ordinate of the point.

2. how far up the screen the dot is. For example, Dot A is at position 800 up the screen. This is often called the Y co-ordinate of the point.

Hence, Dot A has co-ordinates (200,800). Notice that the X co-ordinate is written before the Y co-ordinate.

What are the co-ordinates of Dot B in the diagram?

Type
```
10 MODE 5
20 MOVE 200,800
30 DRAW 800,200
40 END
```

and run the program. You should see a line on the screen, drawn from the top left-hand corner towards the bottom right-hand corner of the screen.

MODE   This command switches the computer into the specified mode, Mode 5 in this case. When the computer is first switched on, it is in Mode 7.

MOVE   This command moves the cursor to the position specified by the co-ordinates, in this case (200,800). This is, of course, our Point A.

DRAW   This command draws a line from the point (800,200) — which is our Point B — to the last point visited (which is Point A: we went there with the MOVE command).

Notice that the line consists of a number of blobs. If you look carefully, each blob is actually a small square. These blobs are called picture elements, or pixels for short. When we tell the computer to light up a particular dot, it actually illuminates the pixel at that point. The size of a pixel varies from mode to mode. Look carefully at the pixels displayed on the screen now, and then go to the next exercise.

- -

List the program. We are now in Mode 5. Notice that the characters are much larger than the characters in Mode 7. This is because there are only 20 characters per line in Mode 5, but 40 per line in Mode 7.

- -

Type
```
10 MODE 4
```

and run the program. The line is again made up of a number of blobs, but each blob is now smaller, and so the line looks much smoother. In Mode 4, there are 320 pixels across the screen, whereas in Mode 5 there are only 160. Hence, Mode 4 pixels are smaller than Mode 5 pixels, and the pictures are correspondingly better. The word resolution is used to describe the quality of graphics. A computer which provides <u>high resolution graphics</u> can draw high quality pictures, because the pixels are smaller.

- -

Type

        10 MODE 5

and run the program. Notice the poorer resolution.

- -

23.3 Colour

Mode 5 has four colours – black, red, yellow and white. When you first switch to Mode 5, characters are printed in white on a black background. Different foreground and background colours can be selected using the COLOUR command.

- -

Type

        MODE 5
        COLOUR 1
        LIST

Your program will be listed as <u>red</u> characters on a <u>black</u> background.

- -

Type

        COLOUR 2
        LIST

Your program will be listed as <u>yellow</u> characters on a <u>black</u> background.

- -

Type

        COLOUR 3
        LIST

Your program will be listed as <u>white</u> characters on a <u>black</u> background.

- -

Type

        COLOUR 0
        LIST

You should see nothing. COLOUR 0 selects a <u>black</u> foreground. As
the background is also black, no characters will be visible.

        COLOUR 0   sets the foreground colour to BLACK
        COLOUR 1   sets the foreground colour to RED
        COLOUR 2   sets the foreground colour to YELLOW
        COLOUR 3   sets the foreground colour to WHITE

If these colours are displayed on a black-and-white screen, they
will appear as different shades of grey.

- -

Type

        COLOUR 129
        LIST

The characters will be <u>black</u> (selected in the previous exercise)
on a <u>red</u> background. If the number in a COLOUR command is 128 or
greater, then the COLOUR command sets the background colour.

        COLOUR 128 sets the background colour to BLACK   (128=128+0)
        COLOUR 129 sets the background colour to RED   (129=128+1)
        COLOUR 130 sets the background colour to YELLOW (130=128+2)
        COLOUR 131 sets the background colour to WHITE   (131=128+3)

Notice that the number used to select a background colour is
simply 128 more than the number used to select the same colour in
foreground.

- -

Type

        COLOUR 130
        LIST

The characters will be <u>black</u> on a <u>yellow</u> background.

- -

Type

        COLOUR 131
        LIST

The characters will be <u>black</u> on a <u>white</u> background.

- -

The COLOUR command changes the colour of the text foreground and background. It cannot be used for Graphics. However, there is a similar command for graphics, and this is the GCOL command. GCOL stands for Graphics COLour.

Type

    15 GCOL 0,1

and run the program. The line drawn on the screen should be red.

- -

Type

    15 GCOL 0,2

and run the program. The line drawn on the screen should be yellow. GCOL is followed by two numbers. The first is normally 0 (it is beyond the scope of this book to explain the purpose of the non-zero values of this first number). The second determines the graphics colour, using the same values as before (1=red, 2=yellow, etc).

- -

Type

    16 GCOL 0,129
    17 CLG

and run the program. A background colour can be set by the GCOL command in much the same way as with the COLOUR command. 129 in the GCOL command sets the background to red. Hence, in this example, you should see a yellow line on a red background. The command in Line 17 clears the screen, and leaves it in the background colour. CLG stands for CLear Graphics.

- -

Type

    CLG

The screen should be cleared, and left in the background colour.

- -

The following program will only work on a Model B BBC computer.

Type

```
NEW
10 MODE 2
20 FOR F=0 TO 7
30    COLOUR F
40    FOR B=0 TO 7
50       IF B=F THEN 110
60       COLOUR 128+B
70       CLS
80       PRINT "FOREGROUND = ";F
90       PRINT "BACKGROUND = ";128+B
100      FOR DELAY=1 TO 4000 : NEXT
110   NEXT B
120 NEXT F
130 END
```

List the program, and check that you have typed it correctly. Now run the program. This program goes through the combinations of background and foreground colours available in Mode 2. Line 50 ignores the cases when the foreground and background colours are the same. Line 100 causes a delay to give you a chance to look at each combination.

- -

Change the 7 in Line 20 to 15, and change the 7 in Line 40 to 15. Now run the program again. This time the flashing colours will also be displayed.

- -

23.4 Low resolution graphics

So far in this unit, we have used BASIC's graphics commands (such as MOVE and DRAW) to draw pictures on the screen. The computer responds by lighting the appropriate pixels on the screen. We have also seen that the total number of pixels available varies from mode to mode. Using the computer in this way is called <u>high resolution graphics</u>. It is possible to create pictures on the screen using text characters. Because there are fewer character positions on the screen than there are pixels, the pictures produced in this way are correspondingly poorer, and so this technique is often called <u>low resolution graphics</u>.

In Mode 7 there are a total of 25x40=1000 character positions on the screen, as shown in the following diagram:

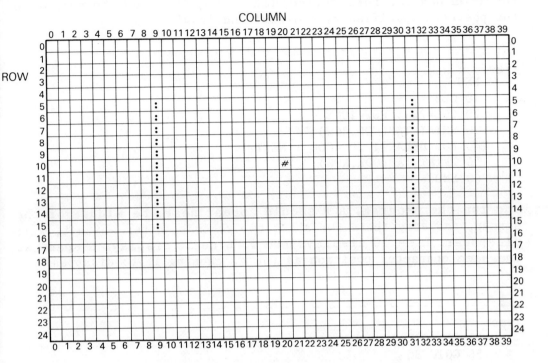

We can select a particular character position by specifying its column and its row. For example:

there is a # at Column 20 Row 10;
there is a : at Column 9 Row 5.

The forty columns are numbered from 0-39, and the twenty-five rows are numbered from 0-24. The top left-hand corner is Column 0, Row 0. The cursor can be moved to any position using the TAB function.

- -

Type

```
10 CLS
20 PRINT TAB(0,0);   "A";
30 PRINT TAB(39,0);  "B";
40 PRINT TAB(0,24);  "C";
50 PRINT TAB(20,10);"#";
60 END
```

and run the program. The letter A should appear in the top left-hand corner, the letter B in the top right-hand corner, the letter C in the bottom left-hand corner, and a # near the middle of the screen. The CLS command clears the screen. The TAB function has the form TAB(column, row); it moves the cursor to the position specified by 'column' and 'row'.

- -

Type
```
NEW
10 CLS
20 COL=20 : ROW=10
30 PRINT TAB(COL,ROW);"#";
40 FOR DELAY=1 TO 4000 : NEXT
50 PRINT TAB(COL,ROW);" "
60 END
```

and run the program. A # should appear near the middle of the screen, and stay there for about two seconds, after which it will disappear. Line 30 displays the #. Line 50 displays a space at the same character position as the #, causing it to disappear.

- -

Type
```
55 COL=COL+1
56 GOTO 30
```

and run the program. The # should now move slowly across the screen. Stop the program after a while by pressing the ESCAPE key. Line 55 increases COL by 1, and Line 56 causes the computer to transfer back to Line 30, which displays the # at the new position. This technique forms the basis of a multitude of computer games. Incidentally, you should NOT use a GOTO to transfer to an earlier line of the program, as we have done here, because it makes programs, especially larger ones, difficult to follow. You should use a REPEAT loop, as shown in the next section.

- -

Type
```
10 REM   BOUNCING #   (BOUNCING1)
20
30 CLS
40 MINCOL=10 : MAXCOL=30
50
60 FOR ROW=5 TO 15
70    PRINT TAB(MINCOL-1,ROW);":";TAB(MAXCOL+1,ROW);":";
80 NEXT ROW
90
100 COL=20 : ROW=10
110 ADDTOCOL=1
```

```
120
130 REPEAT
140    PRINT TAB(COL,ROW);"#";
150    FOR DELAY=1 TO 100 : NEXT
160    PRINT TAB(COL,ROW);" "
170
180    COL=COL+ADDTOCOL
190    IF COL=MINCOL OR COL=MAXCOL THEN ADDTOCOL=-ADDTOCOL
200 UNTIL FALSE
210 END
```

List the program, and make sure that you have typed it correctly. Now run the program. The # bounces backwards and forwards between two walls. Press the ESCAPE key when you wish to terminate the program. Now study the program, and try to understand how it works.

When the # is moving from left to right, ADDTOCOL is +1.

COL is increased by 1 each time Line 180 is executed. When COL is equal to MAXCOL, then ADDTOCOL is set to -1 by Line 190.

COL is now decreased by 1 each time Line 180 is executed, and the # appears to move from right to left. This continues until COL becomes equal to MINCOL, when ADDTOCOL is set back to +1 by Line 190. The # now moves from left to right.

These steps are surrounded by a REPEAT loop which repeats UNTIL FALSE. Since a REPEAT loop continues until the condition is TRUE, and since FALSE can never be true, the loop never ends. You will have to press the ESCAPE key to finish the program.

- -

When the program is working correctly, save it on your cassette as BOUNCING1. Don't forget the 'cassette contents' sheet.

- -

Questions

1.   What new commands have you met in this unit?

2.   What is the difference between text and graphics?

3.   How many modes does the BBC computer have?

4.   Which modes cannot be used on a Model A? Why not?

5.   Which mode provides the most colours?

6.   What is meant by <u>resolution</u>?

7.   Which mode provides the highest resolution graphics?

8.   What is a <u>pixel</u>?

9.   What are <u>co-ordinates</u>?

10. Write a program to draw a <u>red</u> line between point (300,100) and point (700,200).

11. Write a program to draw a triangle made up of <u>yellow</u> lines, with corners at points (300,100), (700,200) and (500,500). The background should be <u>red</u>.

12. Write a program to draw a square made up of <u>red</u> lines on a <u>white</u> background, with opposite corners at points (300,100) and (700,800).

13* Modify the 'bouncing #' program so that the # bounces up and down the screen, as well as from left to right. Vary the values of ROW between 5 and 15. When the program is working correctly, save it on your cassette as BOUNCING2.

24 Sound

The BBC computer can generate sounds through its internal loudspeaker. There are two commands which control the sounds produced – these are SOUND and ENVELOPE. It is beyond the scope of this book to explain all the details of these two commands, because they are quite complex. Only a brief introduction is given here, and the interested reader should consult the User Guide for more detail.

In music, an octave is made up of twelve semitones:

←————— octave —————→   ←————— octave —————→
C C# D D# E F F# G G# A A# B   C C# D D# E F F# G G# A A# B

If we start at C, and play the following twelve semitones (C#, D,... A#, B, C), we will end up at C again. This C, however, is in the next higher octave.

The BBC computer can generate semitones over five full octaves. The SOUND command is used. It has four parameters, and takes the form:

SOUND C, A, P, D

C   is the Channel number. There are FOUR channels (numbered 0, 1, 2 and 3), and each channel can generate one note. All four channels can operate at the same time, because the sound generator is capable of making four sounds at once. We will use Channel 1.

A   is the Amplitude (or loudness). This parameter controls the loudness of the sound, and can be varied between 0 (off) and –15 (loudest).

D   is the Duration of the note (the length of time that the note is emitted). This is in twentieths of a second. Hence, if D is 10, the sound will last 10 twentieths of a second, that is, half a second.

P   is the Pitch of the sound. Having decided what note you want, the value of P to give that note is selected from the following table.

	C	C#	D	D#	E	F	F#	G	G#	A	A#	B
Octave 1	5	9	13	17	21	25	29	33	37	41	45	49
Octave 2	53	57	61	65	69	73	77	81	85	89	93	97
Octave 3	101	105	109	113	117	121	125	129	133	137	141	145
Octave 4	149	153	157	161	165	169	173	177	181	185	189	193
Octave 5	197	201	205	209	213	217	221	225	229	233	237	241

For example,

        C in Octave 1 is produced when P is set at   5;
        D# in Octave 3 is produced when P is set at 113;

Middle C on the piano is produced when P has a value of 53. P can take any whole-number value between 0 and 255. Hence, the BBC computer can play notes one-quarter of a semitone apart.

- -

Type
      SOUND 1,-15, 53, 10
      SOUND 1, -7, 53, 10
      SOUND 1, -1, 53, 10

and compare the sounds produced for different amplitudes.

- -

Type
      SOUND 1,-15, 53, 5
      SOUND 1,-15, 53, 10
      SOUND 1,-15, 53, 20
      SOUND 1,-15, 53, 40

and compare the sounds produced for different durations.

- -

Type

```
10 REM   SOUND DEMONSTRATION    (SOUND1)
20
30 PITCH=5
40 DURATION=10
50 FOR OCTAVE=1 TO 5
60    FOR SEMITONE=1 TO 12
70       PRINT OCTAVE,SEMITONE,PITCH
80       SOUND 1,-15,PITCH,DURATION
90       FOR DELAY=1 TO DURATION*200 : NEXT
100      PITCH=PITCH+4
110   NEXT SEMITONE
120   PRINT
130 NEXT OCTAVE
140 END
```

List the program, and check that you have typed it correctly. Now
run the program. This program plays each semitone from the five
full octaves that the BBC computer can produce. If you look
carefully at the table of P values, you will see that the first
semitone has a P value of 5, and each semitone has a P value 4
more than the previous semitone. The first semitone of an octave
is also 4 more than the last semitone of the previous octave.

In the program, PITCH is initially set to 5 by Line 30. The
note corresponding to this pitch value (C) is sounded by Line 80.
Now the PITCH value is increased by 4 in Line 100, and the loop
is executed again. The note corresponding to the new pitch value
(C#) is sounded by Line 80. This is repeated for the twelve semitones in all five octaves. Line 90 causes the computer to pause
for about one second (DURATION*200=2000, which we saw previously
gave a one-second delay). The duration of a note is only half a
second, and so there is a distinct pause between the notes.

Save the program on your cassette as SOUND1.

- -

A chord in music is the sounding together of several notes. The
BBC computer can play a chord by using several of its channels at
the same time. In the following program, Channel 1 plays C,
Channel 2 plays E, and Channel 3 plays G. To the human ear, the
three notes sound simultaneous. Notice that the computer does not
wait for Channel 1 to finish sounding before going on to execute
the command in Line 20.

Type

```
NEW
10 SOUND 1,-15, 53, 20
20 SOUND 2,-15, 69, 20
30 SOUND 3,-15, 81, 20
```

and run the program.

-- --

Modify the program to become:

```
10 SOUND 1,-15, 53, 20
20 SOUND 1,-15, 69, 20
30 SOUND 1,-15, 81, 20
```

and run the program. The three notes C, E and G are now played on the same channel, and so sound one after the other. Compare this with the previous program.

-- --

Type

```
SOUND 1,-15, 121, 200
```

This command plays an F at maximum loudness for approximately 10 seconds.

-- --

Type

```
NEW
10 ENVELOPE2, 1, 3, -3, 3, 10, 20, 10, 120, 0, 0, -1, 120, 120
20 SOUND 1, 2, 121, 200
```

and run the program. This program produces a sound like a wailing police siren. If you compare the SOUND command here with the SOUND command in the previous exercise, you will see that they are identical, apart from the Amplitude parameter. An amplitude in the range 0 to -15 controls the loudness of the sound. If you use a positive number for the Amplitude (we have used 2 here), it references an ENVELOPE command. In this program, ENVELOPE 2 is defined in Line 10.

   The ENVELOPE command is used with the SOUND command to control the <u>loudness</u> and the <u>pitch</u> of a sound <u>while it is being sounded.</u> Although we have the same basic sound (F) in both these examples, the ENVELOPE command in the latter program modifies the sound while it is playing. The Envelope command is complex to use (it has 14 parameters); for further information, you should consult the User Guide.

-- --

25 Subroutines

25.1 Introduction

In Section 11.3 we developed a program which displayed a histogram on the screen. Histograms could be useful in a number of programs, so it would be helpful to look at this program again, to see whether the commands which displayed the histogram can be used in other programs. We want to be able to identify a group of commands which can be included in any program requiring a histogram. BASIC calls such a group of commands a <u>subroutine</u>.

```
130 REM   HISTOGRAM SUBROUTINE
140 CLS
150 PRINT "CELL FREQ HISTOGRAM"
160 PRINT
170 FOR A1=1 TO NUMBER
180    PRINT ;A1;TAB(5);ADDUP(A1);TAB(10);
190    IF ADDUP(A1)=0 THEN 230
200    FOR A2=1 TO ADDUP(A1)
210       PRINT "*";
220    NEXT A2
230    PRINT
240 NEXT A1
250 RETURN
```

Lines 140–240 are very similar to those in the program in Section 11.3. They assume an ADDUP array has already been defined, and contains values.

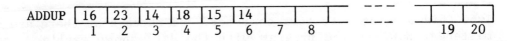

The variable NUMBER tells the subroutine how many of the ADDUP boxes it should use. In this example, NUMBER contains 6.

NUMBER | 6 |

Line 130 is a REMark indicating the start of the subroutine.

Line 250 is a special command which marks the end of a subroutine.

```
 10 REM  HISTOGRAM PROGRAM  (HISTOGRAM1)
 20 DIM ADDUP(20)
 30
 40 INPUT "ENTER NUMBER OF CELLS IN HISTOGRAM ",NUMBER
 50 FOR A1=1 TO NUMBER
 60    PRINT "ENTER VALUE IN CELL ";A1;
 70    INPUT " ",ADDUP(A1)
 80 NEXT A1
 90
100 GOSUB 130
110 END
120
```

Line 20   declares the ADDUP array with 20 boxes.

Line 40   asks the user to enter how many cells there are in the histogram. This number must be in the range 1-20, and specifies how many of the ADDUP boxes will actually be used.

Lines 50-80   establish the values in the ADDUP boxes.

Line 100   is a special command for transferring to a subroutine. GOSUB 130 means GOto the SUBroutine at Line 130. The computer executes the command at Line 130, and continues to execute commands until it encounters a RETURN command. The computer then returns to the line immediately following the line containing the GOSUB. In this example, that would be Line 110.

- -

Type this program into your computer, and check that there are no mistakes. Now run the program with the data shown earlier. Does the program work correctly? Try it with different data.

- -

When the program is working correctly, save it on your cassette as HISTOGRAM1. Don't forget the 'cassette contents' sheet.

- -

25.2 GOSUB and RETURN

- -

Type

NEW
```
10 REM
20 GOSUB 60
30 REM
40 END
```
Main program

50

```
60 REM   START OF SUBROUTINE
70 REM
80 RETURN
```
Subroutine

and list the program. This is a very simple program whose purpose
is to demonstrate 'transfer to' and 'return from' a subroutine.
Line 20 contains the GOSUB command which tells the computer to
start executing the first line of the subroutine (Line 60). This
is known as calling the subroutine. The computer continues
executing the commands of the subroutine until it encounters the
RETURN command in Line 80. At this point it returns to the line
immediately after the line containing the GOSUB command, Line 30
in this case.

- -

Type

TRACE ON
RUN

and check that the commands are executed in the order that you
expect.

- -

Type

35 GOSUB 60

and run the program again. Notice that the subroutine is now
called twice. Each time, the computer begins at Line 60, and
executes Line 70 followed by Line 80. However, when the
subroutine is finished, the computer returns to Line 30 after the
first call, and to Line 40 after the second call. Hence, the
computer remembers the line-number of the line containing the
GOSUB, so that it can return correctly.

- -

Type

    LIST
    RENUMBER
    LIST

and notice that the line-numbers in the GOSUB commands are altered to reflect the change in line-number of the first command of the subroutine.

- -

25.3 The ON...GOSUB command

The ON...GOSUB command allows a particular subroutine out of a group of subroutines to be called, depending on the value of some variable.

- -

Type

```
     10 REPEAT
     20    INPUT "ENTER NUMBER ",K
     30    IF K=0 THEN 60
     40    ON K GOSUB 90,110,130
     50    PRINT
     60 UNTIL K=0
     70 END
     80
     90 PRINT "SUBROUTINE 1"
    100 RETURN
    110 PRINT "SUBROUTINE 2"
    120 RETURN
    130 PRINT "SUBROUTINE 3"
    140 RETURN
```

and run the program, entering values of 1, 2 and 3 when invited to enter a number. The command

    ON K GOSUB 90,110,130

calls the subroutine at Line 90 if K is equal to 1;
calls the subroutine at Line 110 if K is equal to 2;
calls the subroutine at Line 130 if K is equal to 3;

- -

There are only three line-numbers specified in the ON...GOSUB command here (90, 110 and 130). If K does not have a value of 1

or 2 or 3, the computer will not know what to do. Run the program
again, and type 4 when invited to enter a number. The computer
will tell you that you have made a mistake.

- -

```
*************************************************************
*                                                           *
*     The same group of commands is often required more than *
*     once in a program. These commands can be grouped together *
*     to form a subroutine, which can be called from a number *
*     of places in the program.                              *
*                                                           *
*     The same group of commands is often required in several *
*     programs (e.g. the Histogram commands). These commands *
*     can be grouped together to form a subroutine, and the *
*     subroutine saved in a subroutine library on cassette. It *
*     can be included in any program.                        *
*                                                           *
*     A subroutine is called using the GOSUB command.        *
*                                                           *
*     The RETURN command causes the computer to return from a *
*     subroutine, to the line immediately following the line *
*     which called the subroutine.                           *
*                                                           *
*     A large program is often split up into small parts so as *
*     to make it more manageable. Each part can be written as a *
*     subroutine. This is illustrated in Example Program III *
*     in Unit 30. The ON...GOSUB command is also used in this *
*     program.                                               *
*                                                           *
*************************************************************
```

Questions

1.   What new commands have you met in this unit?

2.   Explain what the GOSUB command does.

3.   Explain what the RETURN command does.

4.   What happens if the computer executes the command

         ON X GOSUB 100, 200, 300, 400, 500

     with an X value of   0?   1?   2?   3?   4?   5?   6?

26 Procedures

26.1 Introduction

In the previous unit, we saw that commands can be grouped together to form a subroutine. The GOSUB command is used to <u>call</u> a subroutine, and the RETURN command causes the computer to <u>return</u> from the subroutine to the line immediately following the GOSUB command. BBC BASIC extends the idea of a subroutine by allowing a name to be attached to the group of commands; this name can then be used to call the group of commands. These are called <u>procedures.</u> A procedure has the following form:

```
    DEF PROCprocedure-name
    ...  ⎫
    ...  ⎪
    ...  ⎬  the commands making up the procedure.
    ...  ⎪
    ...  ⎭
    ENDPROC
```

The beginning of a procedure is marked by the DEFine PROCedure command (DEF PROC...); procedure-name is the name that we are attaching to this group of commands. You should choose a name which indicates the purpose of the commands.

The end of a procedure is marked by the END PROCedure command (ENDPROC).

A procedure is called simply by mentioning its name in a line of the program. For example,

```
    100 PROCprocedure-name
```

will call the procedure called 'procedure-name'.

- -

Load the HISTOGRAM1 program from your cassette. List the program, and check that it is correct. Now run the program. Does it produce the correct results?

- -

Type

    100 PROC_HISTOGRAM

    130 DEF PROC_HISTOGRAM
    250 ENDPROC

and list the program. Line 130 defines the procedure called
PROC_HISTOGRAM. To make the name easier to read, we have used the
'underline' character (which is on the same key as the 'pound')
to separate the word PROC from the actual procedure name
(HISTOGRAM). In Mode 7, the 'underline' character looks like a
'minus' when displayed on the screen, so you have to be careful
to use the right character.
　　The procedure is called by Line 100, which simply contains
the name of the procedure. This is equivalent to the GOSUB as
used with subroutines. Notice that there is no RETURN command at
the end of a procedure. When the computer encounters the ENDPROC
command, it returns to the line immediately following the one
which called the procedure, in exactly the same way as with
subroutines.
　　Now run the program. The results should be the same as when
you used a subroutine.

- -

26.2 Calling a procedure

- -

Type

    NEW
    ┌─────────────────────────────────┐
    │ 10 REM   │
    │ 20 PROC_TEST   │   Main program
    │ 30 REM   │
    │ 40 END   │
    └─────────────────────────────────┘

    50

    ┌─────────────────────────────────┐
    │ 60 DEF PROC_TEST   │
    │ 70 REM   │   Procedure
    │ 80 ENDPROC   │
    └─────────────────────────────────┘

and list the program. This is a very simple program whose purpose
is to demonstrate 'transfer to' and 'return from' a procedure.
Line 20 contains the procedure name which tells the computer to
start executing the procedure. This is known as calling the
procedure. The computer executes the commands of the procedure

until it encounters the ENDPROC command in Line 80. At this point it <u>returns</u> to the line immediately after the line which called the procedure, Line 30 in this case.

- -

Type
```
    TRACE ON
    RUN
```

and check that the commands are executed in the order that you expect. Notice that Line 60 (the DEF PROC... line) does not appear in the trace - the first line of the procedure is actually Line 70.

- -

Type
```
    35 PROC_TEST
```

and run the program again. Notice that the procedure is now called twice. Each time, the computer begins at Line 70, and then executes Line 80. However, when the procedure is finished, the computer returns to Line 30 after the first call, and to Line 40 after the second call. Hence, the computer remembers the line-number of the line calling the procedure, so that it can return correctly.

- -

26.3 Parameters

In Unit 21, we used 'parameters' to pass to a function the values that we were asking that function to work on. By varying the values of the parameters, we could control what the function did. The same idea can be used with procedures.

Type
```
    10 TIME=0
    20 PROC_PAUSE(2000)
    30 PRINT TIME DIV 100, TIME MOD 100
    40 END
    50
    60 DEF PROC_PAUSE(DELAY)
    70 FOR K=1 TO DELAY : NEXT
    80 ENDPROC
```

and run the program. The procedure should cause a delay of about 1 second. Lines 60-80 define a procedure called PROC_PAUSE. It has one parameter (DELAY) which is written in brackets following the procedure name. To be precise, the parameters used in the definition of a procedure are called the <u>formal parameters.</u>

The procedure is called in Line 20, with a value of 2000 written in brackets following the procedure name. This number of 2000 is called the <u>actual parameter,</u> because it is the value we want the procedure to work with <u>on this occasion.</u> Before executing the first command of the procedure, the formal parameter (DELAY) is set to the value of the actual parameter (2000). The computer now executes the commands in the procedure, with DELAY having a value of 2000.

- -

Modify Line 20 to become:

        20 PROC_PAUSE(6000)

and run the program again. This time, the procedure is called with a parameter of 6000. Before executing the first command of the procedure, the formal parameter (DELAY) is set to the value of the actual parameter (6000). The computer now executes the commands in the procedure, with DELAY having a value of 6000. Hence, there should be a delay of about 3 seconds.

- -

Type
        15 WAIT=6000
        20 PROC_PAUSE(WAIT)

and run the program again. Notice that the actual parameter may be a variable (we have used WAIT here).

- -

A procedure may have several parameters. In this case, the procedure must be called with the same number of actual parameters as there are formal parameters. When the procedure is called:

        the FIRST formal parameter is set to the value of the FIRST actual parameter. The SECOND formal parameter is set to the value of the SECOND actual parameter. And so on.

The commands making up the procedure are now executed with the formal parameters having these assigned values.

26.4 Local variables

Type

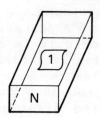

```
10 N=1
20 PRINT "BEFORE ... N = ";N
30 PROC_TEST
40 PRINT "AFTER  ... N = ";N
50 END
60
70 DEF PROC_TEST
80 PRINT "INSIDE ... N = ";N
90 ENDPROC
```

and list the program. Line 10 declares a variable called N, and
sets it to 1. Now run the program. The output should be:

```
BEFORE ... N = 1
INSIDE ... N = 1
AFTER  ... N = 1
```

Lines 20, 40 and 80 display the value of N before the call to
PROC_TEST, after the call to PROC_TEST, and inside PROC_TEST
itself. N is equal to 1 in all three cases. Hence, variables such
as N can be accessed from anywhere in a program, including from
within procedures. They are called global variables.

- -

Type

```
75 N=2
```

and run the program. The output should be:

```
BEFORE ... N = 1
INSIDE ... N = 2
AFTER  ... N = 2
```

The value of N is now changed to 2 inside the procedure. When the
computer returns to the main program, and executes Line 40, N
still contains its new value (2). Hence, the values of global
variables can be changed from anywhere in a program, including
from within a procedure.

- -

Modify the program to become:

```
10 N=1
20 PRINT "BEFORE ... N = ";N
30 PROC_TEST
40 PRINT "AFTER  ... N = ";N
50 END
60
70 DEF PROC_TEST
73 LOCAL N
75 N=2
80 PRINT "INSIDE ... N = ";N
90 ENDPROC
```

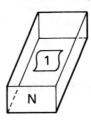

The command N=1 in Line 10 tells the computer to call one of its memory boxes N, and to store the value 1 in that box. Inside the procedure, we have included the command LOCAL N. This command tells the computer to label another of its memory boxes with the same name of N, and to reserve this box for use by the procedure only. In other words, it is <u>local</u> to PROC_TEST. We now have two memory boxes called N - one which is used by the procedure, and one which is used by the main program. The command N=2 in Line 75 stores the value 2 in the procedure's memory box. It has no effect on the other memory box called N. Now run the program. The output should be:

```
BEFORE ... N = 1
INSIDE ... N = 2
AFTER  ... N = 1
```

The LOCAL command allows us to define variables which are local to a procedure. This is very important when writing large programs, because it is easy mistakenly to use the same variable both within and outside a procedure, and to change its value without meaning to. Errors of this nature are very difficult to locate, and can be eliminated by defining ALL variables within a procedure as local variables. The exceptions are parameters, and variables in the main program that you WISH to use.

26.5 An example procedure

The procedure PROC_CIRCLE in the following program will draw a circle on the screen, in Mode 4. Don't worry if you don't understand the details of this program (some of the commands use mathematical functions); we are using it simply to illustrate parameters and local variables.

```
10 REM   CIRCLE PROGRAM   (CIRCLE1)
20
30 MODE 4
40 CLG
50 PROC_CIRCLE(600,500,200)
60 END
70
80 DEF PROC_CIRCLE(XCENTRE, YCENTRE, radius)
90 LOCAL X,Y,K,ANGLE
100 X=XCENTRE
110 Y=YCENTRE+radius
120 MOVE X,Y
130 FOR K=2 TO 360 STEP 2
140    ANGLE=K*PI/180
150    X=XCENTRE+radius*SIN(ANGLE)
160    Y=YCENTRE+radius*COS(ANGLE)
170    DRAW X,Y
180 NEXT K
190 ENDPROC
```

There are THREE formal parameters:

XCENTRE and YCENTRE, which are the X and Y co-ordinates of the centre of the circle;

radius, which is the radius of the circle. Note that radius is in small letters, to avoid confusion with RAD.

There are FOUR variables (X, Y, K and ANGLE) which are used only inside the procedure. Hence they are made LOCAL in Line 90.

The procedure is called in Line 50 with THREE actual parameters:

600, which is assigned to XCENTRE;
500, which is assigned to YCENTRE;
200, which is assigned to radius.

The commands within the procedure are now executed.

Type the program into your computer. List it to make sure that you have typed it correctly. Now run the program. You should see a circle drawn on the screen. Try changing the actual parameters in Line 50. From this you should realise how powerful this procedure is when you want to draw many circles at different places on the screen.

When the program is working correctly, save it on your cassette as CIRCLE1.

26.6 User-defined functions

In Unit 21 we saw that there are a number of built-in functions in BASIC, for example MID$, LEN and RND. In addition to these functions, BBC BASIC also permits you to define your own functions. These are called <u>user-defined functions</u>, because it is the user who defines them. They are very similar to procedures, but there is one major difference:

A FUNCTION RETURNS A VALUE; A PROCEDURE DOES NOT.

A function has the following form:

```
DEF FNfunction-name
...  ⎫
...  ⎪
...  ⎬   the commands making up the function.
...  ⎪
...  ⎭
= value
```

The beginning of a function is marked by the DEFine FUNCTION command (DEF FN...); function-name is the name that we are attaching to this group of commands. You should choose a name which indicates the purpose of the commands.

The end of a function is marked by the '= value' command. This sets the value that is to be returned by the function.

A function is called simply by mentioning its name as part of a line of the program. For example,

```
120 PRINT FNfunction-name
```

will call the function called 'function-name', and then print the value returned by the function. If the function returns a string, then the function can be used wherever a normal string is allowed. If the function returns a number, then the function can be used wherever a normal number is allowed.

The following program is one possible solution to Question 11 at the end of Unit 17. It illustrates a user-defined function.

```
 10 INPUT "ENTER STRING ",X$
 20 PRINT "NEW STRING  = ";FN_CONVERT_TO_CAPITALS(X$)
 30 END
 40
 50 DEF FN_CONVERT_TO_CAPITALS(A$)
 60 LOCAL B$,K,N
 70 B$=""
 80 IF A$="" THEN 140
 90 FOR K=1 TO LEN(A$)
100    N=ASC(MID$(A$,K,1))
110    IF N>=97 AND N<=122 THEN N=N-32
120    B$=B$+CHR$(N)
130 NEXT K
140 =B$
```

The following notes may help you to understand the program:

Line 50   defines a user function. Its purpose is to convert small letters to capital letters in a string which is passed to it as a parameter. A$ is the formal parameter.

Line 20   The function is called by mentioning its name as part of a line. The actual parameter used in this example is X$; this is copied into the formal parameter A$ when the function is called.

Lines 90–130   make up a FOR loop which copies each character of A$ into B$, with small letters being converted into capitals. The method used is the same as that described in Appendix A, in the answer to Question 11, Unit 17.

Line 140   returns the string in B$. This is printed out in the main program by Line 20.

- -

Type the program into your computer. List it and check that you have typed it correctly. Now run the program. Does it perform correctly?

- -

26.7 Single-line functions

A function may have no commands between the 'DEF FN...' command
and the '= value' command, in which case it can be written on one
line. This is known as a single-line function. An example of a
single-line function with one parameter (AGE) is:

    DEF FN_CALCULATE_PAY(AGE)=5*AGE+20

Type

    10 INPUT "ENTER AGE ",AGE
    20 PRINT "POCKET MONEY = ";FN_CALCULATE_PAY(AGE)
    30 END
    40
    50 DEF FN_CALCULATE_PAY(AGE)=5*AGE+20

and run the program. Does it perform correctly? Notice that the
formal parameter and the actual parameter can have the same name.
    BBC BASIC provides both single-line functions (described
here) and multi-line functions (described in Section 26.6). Most
versions of BASIC provide only single-line functions.

26.8 Comparison of subroutines and procedures

Functions and Procedures must be placed at the end of a program.

    A program which is constructed using procedures is usually
easier to understand than one constructed from subroutines. This
is because a subroutine is called by the 'GOSUB line-number'
command whereas a procedure is called by the 'PROCprocedure-name'
command. Hence, if you choose names which reflect the purposes of
the procedures, your programs will be easy to understand. The
command 'GOSUB line-number', on the other hand, doesn't give you
any idea what the subroutine does. Therefore, it is good practice
when you are using subroutines to put a REMark near to the GOSUB
command, explaining the purpose of the subroutine.
    You usually need to pass values to a subroutine or a
procedure, for it to work on. The parameters provided with
procedures make this simple. On the other hand, if you are using
subroutines, you will have to use global variables, which can
lead to errors unless you are very careful.
    All variables are global to subroutines. Procedures allow
local variables. Those variables which are used only in a
procedure should be made local to that procedure. By doing so,
you eliminate any problems which may arise from using a variable
of the same name in another part of the program.

Example Program II in Unit 27 illustrates a program constructed using procedures. Example Program III in Unit 30 illustrates a program constructed using subroutines.

Questions

1.   What new commands have you met in this unit?

2.   How do you define a procedure?

3.   How do you call a procedure?

4.   What are formal parameters? What are actual parameters?

5.   What are local variables? How do you use them?

6.   How do you define a user-defined function?

7.   How do you call a user-defined function?

8.   What is the difference between a procedure and a user-defined function?

9*   What output will the following program produce?

```
10 FOR K=1 TO 2
20    PRINT "OUTSIDE   K = ";K
30    PROC_EXAMPLE
40 NEXT K
50 PRINT "FINISHED"
60 END
70
80 DEF PROC_EXAMPLE
90 FOR K=1 TO 3
100    PRINT "INSIDE   K = ";K
112 NEXT K
120 ENDPROC
```

10.   Delete Lines 10-60 from the previous program, and then run it again. Can you explain the error message? (Hint: the commands of the procedure are now executed without the procedure being called in the usual way).

27 Example Program II

27.1 Background

In the local primary school in YOURTOWN, one teacher looks after
the children who have just started school. This teacher has asked
you to develop a computer program which will help these children
learn the letters of the alphabet. The program is to be in the
form of a game which involves the child shooting at the letters
with a gun. The twenty-six letters of the alphabet are to be
displayed randomly in one part of the screen. The child can move
a gun displayed on the screen to point at an individual letter,
and can shoot bullets at that letter. The letters are to be shot
in alphabetical order ('a' first, 'b' second, and so on). If the
correct letter is hit, it disappears from the screen, and the
child goes on to the next letter. The time that has elapsed since
the child started is to be displayed on the screen, in minutes
and seconds. The game is complete when the child has shot all
twenty-six letters. In case the child should forget how far he
has got, the letters already shot are to be displayed in another
part of the screen.

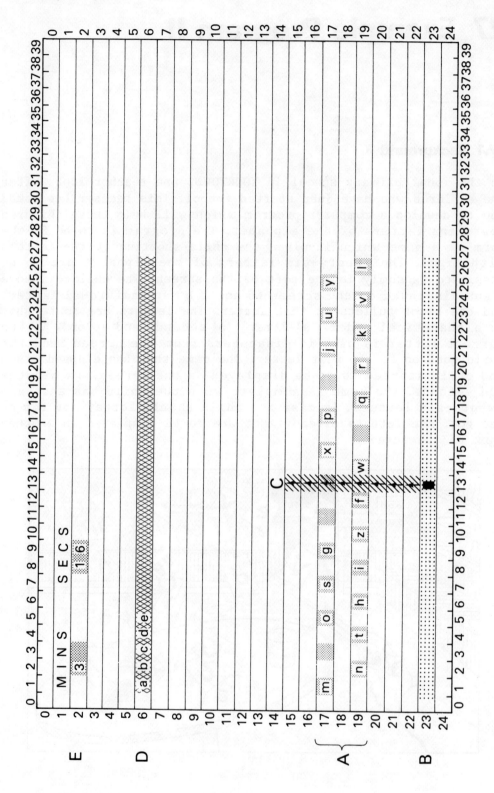

27.2 The layout of the screen

A possible screen layout for this program is shown in Figure 27.1. There are 40 columns across the screen, numbered 0–39, and there are 25 rows down the screen, numbered 0–24. Altogether, there are 40x25=1000 positions on the screen, and any one position is specified by stating its 'column' and its 'row'. For example:

        the character at Column 3   Row 6 is 'c';
        the character at Column 25   Row 17 is 'y';
        the gun is at   Column 13   Row 23.

There are five regions of the screen which are important to this program; they are marked A, B, C, D, and E.

A   There are twenty-six character positions in this region. The twenty-six letters of the alphabet are scattered at random into these positions. As a letter is shot, it is removed from the screen, and replaced by a space. The letters could have been displayed on one row, but they alternate between two rows to make them easier to read.

B   This region shows the positions to which the gun can be moved. The gun always remains in Row 23, but it can be moved anywhere between Column 1 and Column 26. The gun is moved one position to the left by the child pressing the 'left-arrow' on the keyboard, and one position to the right by the child pressing the 'right-arrow' key. The gun is fired by the child pressing the 'space' bar.

C   The gun fires bullets. These bullets are represented on the screen as 'arrows', which are shown in this region. If a bullet hits the current letter, that letter is removed from the screen. The arrows only appear on the screen when the gun is fired. This region moves with the gun, so that the bullets always appear to come from the gun.

D   The letters that have been shot appear in this region.

E   The time that has passed since the child started playing is displayed in this region, in minutes and seconds. The numbers continually change as time passes.

27.3 The important data items within the program

The next step is to describe the data items that are needed in the program to provide the information displayed in these five regions of the screen.

ALPHABET$ is a string variable which holds the letters of the alphabet in their correct order.

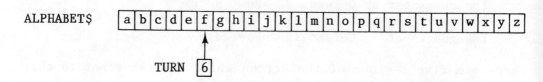

ALPHABET$

TURN is a variable which keeps track of the letter that the child is shooting at. On his first turn (TURN=1), the child will be shooting at the letter 'a'. On his second turn (TURN=2), he will be shooting at the letter 'b'. And so on. When TURN is equal to 6, as here, the child is shooting at the letter 'f'.

DISPLAYED$ is a string array containing 26 boxes. The letters of ALPHABET$ are scattered at random into this array.

```
        1   3   5   7   9  11  13  15  17  19  21  23  25
DISPLAYED$  m n a t o h s i g z e f c w x b p q d r j k u v y l
          2   4   6   8  10  12  14  16  18  20  22  24  26
```

Let us now see how these variables are used to provide the data displayed in the five regions on the screen.

A   The letters displayed in this region come from the DISPLAYED$ array.

        Column 1 Row 17 comes from DISPLAYED$(1)
        Column 2 Row 19 comes from DISPLAYED$(2)
        Column 3 Row 17 comes from DISPLAYED$(3)
       .Column 4 Row 19 comes from DISPLAYED$(4)
            and so on

    Notice that the column number is exactly the same as the subscript of the DISPLAYED$ array. Odd boxes of DISPLAYED$ go into Row 17, even boxes into Row 19.

B   The gun is displayed on the screen at the position specified
       by the two variables GUNCOL and GUNROW. When a 'left-arrow'
       is detected from the keyboard, GUNCOL is reduced by 1, and
       the gun displayed at the new position. When a 'right-arrow'
       is detected from the keyboard, GUNCOL is increased by 1, and
       the gun displayed at the new position. GUNROW is fixed. The
       gun is not allowed to move outside this region.

C   When the 'space bar' is pressed, the gun fires bullets up
       the screen. The gun is in the correct position if

           DISPLAYED$(GUNCOL) = the TURNth character of ALPHABET$

       If the gun is in the correct column, the letter in that
       column is erased by setting DISPLAYED$(GUNCOL) to a space.

D   The letters already shot are simply the letters from the
       start of ALPHABET$ up to, and including, the TURNth letter.
       They are displayed after a letter has been shot, so the
       TURNth letter is included. In this example, the letters are
       'abcde' because these were the letters that had been shot at
       the end of Turn 5. The player is now on Turn 6, but he has
       not yet shot the 'f'.

E   The figures displayed here are obtained by converting the
       value in the TIME variable to minutes and seconds. TIME is
       set to zero at the start of the program.

27.4 The program itself

Having described the layout of the screen, and the data items
within the program which provide values for the screen, the next
step is to describe the program itself. In a sense, you can think
of the program as simply changing the values in these data items,
which, in turn, causes the values on the screen to change. The
program can be explained in terms of a number of steps:

Step 1 :   display the letters to be shot (in Region A).

Step 2 :   display the time (in Region E).

Step 3 :   check whether a key has been pressed. If it is a 'left-arrow', then move the gun one position to the left (in Region B). If it is a 'right-arrow', then move the gun one position to the right (in Region B). If it is a 'space', then fire the gun (in Region C).

Steps 2 and 3 are repeated until the correct letter is shot.

Step 4 :   display the letters shot (in Region D).

These FOUR steps are repeated for each of the twenty-six letters of the alphabet. We will use procedures to represent the four steps in our program. An outline of the program follows:

```
40 FOR TURN=1 TO NUMBER
50     PROC_DISPLAY_LETTERS_TO_SHOOT
60
70     HIT$="NO"
80     REPEAT
90        PROC_DISPLAY_TIME
100        PROC_PROCESS_KEYS
110     UNTIL HIT$="YES"
120
130     PROC_DISPLAY_LETTERS_SHOT
140 NEXT TURN
```

Line 50   : This procedure carries out Step 1.
Line 90   : This procedure carries out Step 2.
Line 100   : This procedure carries out Step 3.

Lines 80,110 : This REPEAT loop causes Steps 2 and 3 to be repeated until the correct letter is shot.

Line 130   : This procedure carries out Step 4.

Lines 40,140 : This FOR loop causes the four steps to be repeated for the twenty-six letters of the alphabet.

A complete listing of the program is included in the following pages. It has been written using procedures, in a way which is intended to be more-or-less self-explanatory.

PRACTICAL EXERCISES

- -

Study the program listing carefully, and try to understand how it works. Notice that the procedures are in alphabetical order, so that any one procedure is easy to find.

- -

Type the program into your computer. List it, and make sure that you have typed it correctly. Now save it on your cassette as SHOOT1.

- -

Run the program, and check that it performs correctly. If not, correct it, and save the corrected version on your cassette.

- -

Modify the program so that it keeps track of how many times the child shoots at a wrong letter. At the end of the game, penalise the child by ten seconds for each mistake he or she made. When the program is working correctly, save it on your cassette as SHOOT2.

- -

Modify ALPHABET$ to be 'abcde'. Study the program to see why it still works correctly.

- -

It is sometimes difficult to align the gun in the right column; it would be easier if the gun was positioned closer to the letters. Modify the program so that the gun is displayed in Row 21, instead of Row 23 as at present.

- -

The full listing of the program is on the following three pages.

```
 10 REM   SHOOT_THE_ALPHABET   (SHOOT1)
 20
 30 PROC_INITIALISE
 40 FOR TURN=1 TO NUMBER
 50    PROC_DISPLAY_LETTERS_TO_SHOOT
 60
 70    HIT$="NO"
 80    REPEAT
 90       PROC_DISPLAY_TIME
100       PROC_PROCESS_KEYS
110    UNTIL HIT$="YES"
120
130    PROC_DISPLAY_LETTERS_SHOT
140 NEXT TURN
150 PROC_FINALISE
160 END
170
180 REM-----------------------------------------------------
190 DEF PROC_ARROWS(YLAST)
200 FOR Y=GUNROW-1 TO YLAST STEP -1
210   PRINT TAB(GUNCOL,Y);ARROW$
220   PROC_PAUSE(400)
230   PRINT TAB(GUNCOL,Y);" "
240 NEXT Y
250 ENDPROC
260
270 REM-----------------------------------------------------
280 DEF PROC_PAUSE(DELAY)
290 FOR K=1 TO DELAY : NEXT
300 ENDPROC
310
320 REM-----------------------------------------------------
330 DEF PROC_DISPLAY_LETTERS_SHOT
340 PRINT TAB(1,6);LEFT$(ALPHABET$,TURN)
350 ENDPROC
360
370 REM-----------------------------------------------------
380 DEF PROC_DISPLAY_LETTERS_TO_SHOOT
390 FOR K=1 TO NUMBER
400    PRINT TAB(K, 19-(K MOD 2)*2);DISPLAYED$(K)
410 NEXT K
420 ENDPROC
430
440 REM-----------------------------------------------------
450 DEF PROC_DISPLAY_TIME
460 T=TIME DIV 100
470 PRINT TAB(2,2);T DIV 60;TAB(8,2);T MOD 60;" "
480 ENDPROC
```

```
490
500 REM----------------------------------------------------
510 DEF PROC_FINALISE
520 *FX 4,0                    :REM RESTORE CURSOR EDITING
530 ENDPROC
540
550 REM----------------------------------------------------
560 DEF PROC_HIT
570 FOR K=5 TO 45 STEP 8
580    SOUND 1,-15,K,1
590 NEXT K
600 ENDPROC
610
620 REM----------------------------------------------------
630 DEF PROC_INITIALISE
640 DIM DISPLAYED$(26)
650 *FX4,1                     :REM DISABLE CURSOR EDITING
660 ALPHABET$="abcdefghijklmnopqrstuvwxyz"
670 NUMBER=LEN(ALPHABET$)
680 PROC_RANDOMISE_LETTERS_IN_DISPLAYED_ARRAY
690 GUN$=CHR$(124)
700 ARROW$=CHR$(94)
710 GUNCOL=NUMBER DIV 2
720 GUNROW=23
730 CLS
740 PRINT TAB(1,1);"MINS";TAB(7,1);"SECS"
750 PRINT TAB(GUNCOL,GUNROW);GUN$
760 TIME=0
770 ENDPROC
780
790 REM----------------------------------------------------
800 DEF PROC_LEFT
810 IF GUNCOL=1 THEN 850
820 PRINT TAB(GUNCOL,GUNROW);" "
830 GUNCOL=GUNCOL-1
840 PRINT TAB(GUNCOL,GUNROW);GUN$
850 ENDPROC
860
870 REM----------------------------------------------------
880 DEF PROC_MISS
890 SOUND 1,-15,5,6
900 ENDPROC
910
```

```
 920 REM-----------------------------------------------------------
 930 DEF PROC_PROCESS_KEYS
 940 X$=INKEY$(20)
 950 IF X$=CHR$(136) THEN PROC_LEFT
 960 IF X$=CHR$(137) THEN PROC_RIGHT
 970 IF X$=" "        THEN PROC_SHOOT
 980 ENDPROC
 990
1000 REM-----------------------------------------------------------
1010 DEF PROC_RANDOMISE_LETTERS_IN_DISPLAYED_ARRAY
1020 TEMP$=ALPHABET$
1030 FOR K=1 TO NUMBER
1040    R=RND(LEN(TEMP$))
1050    DISPLAYED$(K)=MID$(TEMP$,R,1)
1060    TEMP$=LEFT$(TEMP$,R-1)+RIGHT$(TEMP$,LEN(TEMP$)-R)
1070 NEXT K
1080 ENDPROC
1090
1100 REM-----------------------------------------------------------
1110 DEF PROC_RIGHT
1120 IF GUNCOL=NUMBER THEN 1160
1130 PRINT TAB(GUNCOL,GUNROW);" "
1140 GUNCOL=GUNCOL+1
1150 PRINT TAB(GUNCOL,GUNROW);GUN$
1160 ENDPROC
1170
1180 REM-----------------------------------------------------------
1190 DEF PROC_SHOOT
1200 IF DISPLAYED$(GUNCOL)=MID$(ALPHABET$,TURN,1) THEN 1250
1210    PROC_ARROWS(16)
1220    PROC_MISS
1230    PROC_DISPLAY_LETTERS_TO_SHOOT
1240 GOTO 1290
1250    PROC_ARROWS(19-(GUNCOL MOD 2)*2)
1260    PROC_HIT
1270    HIT$="YES"
1280    DISPLAYED$(GUNCOL)=" "
1290 REM END-IF
1300 ENDPROC
```

28 Data files

28.1 Introduction

Up to now, all the data required by a program has been either contained within the program itself, or been entered via the keyboard in response to the computer executing an INPUT command. This unit describes how data can be stored on cassette by a program, and read from cassette by a program.

The data belonging to one particular program will be grouped together on one part of the tape. This group of data is called a 'file'. A file is simply a collection of related data items. For example, a file might contain data about a group of children:

	FIRST-NAME	LAST-NAME	TYPE	AGE
1	JOHN	SMITH	BOY	10
2	SUSAN	GREAVES	GIRL	11
3	ALISON	JONES	GIRL	9
4	JOHN	DAVIS	BOY	9
5	MARTIN	COATS	BOY	9
6	DAVID	DAVIS	BOY	12

There are FOUR pieces of information on each child: its first-name, its last-name, its age, and whether that child is a boy or a girl. The four data items relating to a particular child make up a record. For example,

```
Record 1 is   JOHN     SMITH   BOY    10
Record 3 is   ALISON   JONES   GIRL    9
```

An individual data item, such as FIRST-NAME or LAST-NAME, is called a field of the record.

```
**************************************************************
*                                                            *
*    A file is a collection of records which are related to  *
*    each other.                                             *
*                                                            *
*    A record is a collection of fields (data items).        *
*                                                            *
**************************************************************
```

28.2 Writing to a file

This section describes how a program can create a CHILDREN file
on cassette, and store data in it. In some ways, computer files
are similar to books:

1. before you can read a book, or write in a book, you
    must first OPEN the book;
2. when you have finished reading from a book, or writing
    in a book, you CLOSE the book;
3. you tell what is in a book by looking at the TITLE,
    which is normally written on the outside front cover.

Before you can write to a computer file, you must first open the
file, using a command of the form:

    F1=OPENOUT("CHILDREN")

OPENOUT   means OPEN the file for OUTPUT i.e. the program will
           write data into the file.

CHILDREN   is the name of this file - this is similar to the title
           of a book.

F1   is a numeric variable used in the program to refer to
           the file. If you should open a second file within the
           same program, then use a variable name of F2 (F3 for
           the third file, and so on).

Once the file has been opened, you can write data into it using a
PRINT command.

    PRINT #F1, FIRST$, LAST$, TYPE$, AGE

This command will write the contents of the FIRST$ box, the
contents of the LAST$ box, the contents of the TYPE$ box, and the
contents of the AGE box to the cassette. The #F1 tells the

computer that these values belong to the CHILDREN file, because F1 was linked to the CHILDREN file by the OPENOUT command. In fact, whenever you wish to refer to the CHILDREN file within the program, you use F1.

When you have finished with a file, you must <u>close</u> it, just as you close a book. The command is of the form:

    CLOSE #F1

- -

Type
```
 10 REM  MAKE "CHILDREN" FILE   (CHILDMAKE1)
 20
 30 F1=OPENOUT("CHILDREN")
 40 READ NUMBER
 50 PRINT #F1,NUMBER
 60
 70 FOR K=1 TO NUMBER
 80    READ FIRST$,LAST$,TYPE$,AGE
 90    PRINT #F1,FIRST$,LAST$,TYPE$,AGE
100 NEXT K
110 CLOSE #F1
120 PRINT "CHILDREN FILE CREATED"
130
140 DATA 6
150 DATA "JOHN","SMITH","BOY",10
160 DATA "SUSAN","GREAVES","GIRL",11
170 DATA "ALSION","JONES","GIRL",9
180 DATA "JOHN","DAVIS","BOY","9
190 DATA "MARTIN","COATS","BOY",9
200 DATA "DAVID","COATS","BOY",12
210 END
```

List the program, and check that you have typed it correctly. BEFORE you run the program, save it on your cassette as CHILDMAKE1.

- -

Put a blank cassette into your tape recorder – this will be your 'data' cassette. Now run the program. When the file is opened, the message 'RECORD then RETURN' will appear on the screen. The procedure is the same as when you are saving programs on cassette – simply position the tape to where you want to save the file, press the RECORD button on your recorder, and press the RETURN key on the keyboard. If the program works correctly, the message CHILDREN FILE CREATED should be displayed on the screen. Take the 'data' tape out of the recorder.
- -

28.3 Reading from a file

- -

Type

```
 10 REM   READ "CHILDREN" FILE   (CHILDREAD1)
 20
 30 PRINT "POSITION CASSETTE AT CHILDREN FILE"
 40 PRINT "THEN PRESS THE   -PLAY-   BUTTON"
 50 PRINT
 60 F1=OPENIN("CHILDREN")
 70 INPUT #F1,NUMBER
 80
 90 FOR K=1 TO NUMBER
100    INPUT #F1,FIRST$,LAST$,TYPE$,AGE
110    PRINT FIRST$,LAST$,TYPE$,AGE
120 NEXT K
130 CLOSE #F1
140 PRINT "CHILDREN FILE READ"
150 END
```

List the program and check that you have typed it correctly.
BEFORE you run the program, save it on your 'program' cassette
(not your 'data' cassette) as CHILDREAD1.

- -

Now put the 'data' cassette into your tape recorder and run the
program. If your program works correctly, information about the
six children in the file should be displayed on the screen,
followed by the message CHILDREN FILE READ.

Line 60   The CHILDREN file is OPENED for INPUT, i.e. the program
           reads data from the file.

Line 70   The INPUT #F1 command will read the first data item in
           the CHILDREN file, and store it in the memory box
           called NUMBER. This should be 6, telling the program
           that there are six children records in this file.

Line 100   This INPUT #F1 command reads the next four data items
           in the CHILDREN file, and stores them in FIRST$, LAST$,
           TYPE$, and AGE. These four data items make up one
           record. As with READ and DATA commands, the data on the
           tape must be the same type as the memory box into which
           it will be stored. The computer will tell you that you
           have made a mistake if, for example, you try to store
           "JONES" in the AGE memory box.

- -

Type

```
     90  REPEAT
    120  UNTIL EOF#F1
```

and run the program again. The same children information should be displayed on the screen. EOF stands for End Of File. When the last record of the #F1 file (i.e. the CHILDREN file) has been read, then EOF#F1 is true, and the loop terminates. At all other times EOF#F1 is false, and the loop repeats.

Compare this with the previous version, where we recorded on the tape the fact that there were six records in the file, and our FOR loop repeated six times. In the modified version we don't need to know how many records there are in the file - we simply keep looping until we reach the end of the file.

Questions

1.   What is a <u>file</u>?   A <u>record</u>?   A <u>field</u>?

2.   Write a command to open for output a file called PRODUCTS.

3.   Write a command to open for input a file called CUSTOMERS. This command is to be used in the same program as the command you wrote in answering Question 2.

4.   What is meant by <u>End Of File</u>?

5.   What command would you use to detect that the end of the CUSTOMERS file had been reached?

6.   What command is used to write data to a file?

7.   What command is used to read data from a file?

8.   What must a program do when it has finished using a file?

9.   Write a command to close the CUSTOMERS file.

29 Testing and debugging

29.1 Testing

The purpose of testing is to verify that your program performs as
you think it should. Testing is normally carried out by running
the program with sets of test data, and comparing the actual
results with the results that you expect the program to produce.
An individual set of test data is often called a test case. The
following test cases were used to test the cross-country program
described in Unit 12:

Test case	: 1
Purpose	: To run the program with data from an actual cross-country run.
RUNNERS	: 9 3 14 7 1 15 8 10 2 5 4 6 11 13 12
Expected result	: ARNSIDE 37 BROOKVALE 32 CROFT 51
Test case	: 2
Purpose	: For one team to finish with the minimum score and another team with the maximum score.
RUNNERS	: 1 2 3 4 5 6 7 8 9 10 11 12 13 14 15
Expected result	: ARNSIDE 15 BROOKVALE 40 CROFT 65
Test case	: 3
Purpose	: For all teams to finish with the same total score.
RUNNERS	: 6 1 11 7 2 12 8 3 13 14 4 15 9 5 10
Expected result	: ARNSIDE 40 BROOKVALE 40 CROFT 40
Test case	: 4
Purpose	: To see what the program will do with invalid data.
RUNNERS	: 16 11 21 17 12 22 18 13 23 24 14 25 19 15 20
Expected result	: program should terminate with an error.
Test case	: 5
Purpose	: To see what the program will do if you enter the same runner more than once.
RUNNERS	: 1 1 1 1 1 1 1 1 1 1 1 1 1 1 1
Expected result	: ARNSIDE 120 BROOKVALE 0 CROFT 0

The program is run with each test case in turn, and the output from the program compared with the expected results. In some cases, the program will not perform as we expect. We call this an error. Possible reasons are:

1. Our expectation is wrong - perhaps we made a mistake in our calculations.
2. There is a fault (bug) in the program.

We must first check that our expectation is indeed correct. If not, it should be revised. If the error persists, then we must search the program for the fault causing the error, and eliminate it. This process is known as debugging. It is similar in many ways to what a doctor does to diagnose an illness. If you have a sore throat, a headache, and are covered in spots, you will probably pay a visit to your doctor. He will examine you closely, and take notes of your abnormal conditions - these are known as symptoms. Using these symptoms as clues, he will diagnose (work out) that you have a particular illness (perhaps measles). In programming:

ERRORS   are similar to SYMPTOMS (spots, pain);
BUGS   are similar to ILLNESSES (measles, appendicitis);
DEBUGGING is similar to DIAGNOSIS (identifying the illness).

Recognising errors is an essential factor in testing. It depends both on how good the programmer is, and on the VISIBILITY of the errors. Errors which are clearly visible are more likely to be noticed. It is good practice, therefore, to include additional testing statements in a program when it is written. The purpose of the statements is to show the values contained in important data items. This information is used by the programmer to satisfy himself that the program is performing as he expects. We saw several examples of testing statements in Unit 12.
    You should select test cases which cause:

1. Every command in the program to be executed at least once.
2. Every condition in the program to be executed at least once in both its senses. For example, if the command IF X=1 THEN 90 appeared in our program, we could as a minimum select test cases of:

        X=1   to test the TRUE case;
        X=2 say, to test the FALSE case.

In addition, you should use your knowledge of the problem to guide you in selecting test cases.

29.2 Debugging

Debugging is concerned with locating a fault in the program. It can often take a long time, and so a methodical approach helps.

1.   Study the error carefully, and make a clue-list (on a sheet of paper rather than in your head) of

   WHAT has gone wrong;
   WHEN the error occurred (and when it did not);
   WHERE in the program did it occur;
   TO WHAT EXTENT was the output wrong.

2.   Based on this clue-list, and on your experience, think of possible faults that could cause these symptoms.

3.   Check the program for each of these possibilities, and see if the fault exists. If no fault is found, go back to Step 1, and review the clue-list. Otherwise

4.   Correct the fault, and rerun the program. Make sure that the error has disappeared.

Sometimes you don't have enough information to help you to find the fault. In this case you may need to use a debugging aid. Often, you will know that the program is correct at point X in the program, and incorrect at point Z. The following information could be useful:

1.   Knowing the actual commands executed by the computer between point X and point Z.

2.   The values of particular variables at point X, at point Z, and at selected points between X and Z.

BBC BASIC provides a TRACE facility which shows you the commands that have been executed by the computer. In addition you can insert extra PRINT commands in the program to find out what is held in the variables that interest you. These commands are removed when you have found the bug.

Questions

1.   What is meant by testing?

2.   What is a test case?

3.   What is the difference between an error and a fault?

4.   What is meant by debugging?

5.   What debugging aids have you met?

The following is a solution to Question 6 of Unit 10:

```
10 REM  FOOTBALL RESULTS  (FOOTBALL1)
20
30 REPEAT
40    INPUT "HOME TEAM GOALS ",HOME
50    INPUT "VISITORS  GOALS ",VISITORS
60
70    IF HOME=VISITORS THEN PRINT "DRAW"
80
90    IF HOME>VISITORS THEN PRINT "HOME WIN"
                       ELSE PRINT "AWAY WIN"
100
110    PRINT
120 UNTIL HOME<0
130 END
```

6*   What test cases would you use to test this program?

7.   There is a bug in this program. Did your test cases produce correct answers?

8.   Debug the program. Do your test cases now perform correctly?

9*   Modify the program so that it finishes as soon as you enter a minus value for the number of home goals (you don't have to enter the visitors goals as well).

30 Example Program III

30.1 Background

One of the local schools in YOURTOWN has its own computer. This computer is mainly used in class by the teachers to support their teaching, and to get the children familiar with computers. The headmaster realises the potential of computers, and would like to use his computer to keep information about the children in the school. However, he knows little about computers, and even less about programming, and so he has asked you to help.

At present, the headmaster has a card for each child in the school:

```
First name  :  JOHN
Last  name  :  SMITH
Sex         :  BOY
Age         :  10
```

These cards are kept in a card-box in the headmaster's office. The cards are used on a number of occasions:

Additions. When a child starts at the school, the headmaster makes out a new card, and puts it into the card-box.

Deletions. When a child leaves the school, the headmaster takes that child's card from the card-box, and throws it away.

Changes. Occasionally, the information on a card is wrong; for example, a child's name may have been spelt incorrectly. When this happens, the headmaster retrieves the card from the card-box, corrects it, and then returns the card to the card-box.

Sorting. It is easier to find the card of a particular child if the cards are arranged in alphabetical order. The cards sometimes become disordered, and the headmaster then has to sort them into their correct order.

Selecting. On occasions, the headmaster needs to select all the children who satisfy some conditions – perhaps he needs to know the BOYS who are 9 years old. To do this, he first picks out from the card-box all the cards corresponding to BOYS. Then he goes through these cards, picking out those who are aged nine.

The headmaster has asked you to produce a computer system which will perform the same functions as his card system. We shall call it the 'School Information System', and hereafter refer to it as SIS.

30.2 Designing the computer system

We can use a computer <u>file</u> to hold all the information that is needed on the children. Let us call it the CHILDREN file. As we saw in Unit 28, a file is simply a collection of <u>records</u>. In this example, each record contains the information about ONE child. Hence, we need one record for each child in the school.

		FIRST-NAME	LAST-NAME	TYPE	AGE
Record	1	JOHN	SMITH	BOY	10
Record	2	SUSAN	GREAVES	GIRL	11
Record	3	ALISON	JONES	GIRL	9
Record	4	JOHN	DAVIS	BOY	9
Record	5	MARTIN	COATS	BOY	9
Record	6	DAVID	COATS	BOY	12
......	.	....	.....	...	..
Record	10	....	.....	...	..

The CHILDREN file

Comparing the computer system with the existing card system:

a <u>record</u> is equivalent to a <u>card</u>;

the CHILDREN <u>file</u> is equivalent to the <u>box of cards</u>.

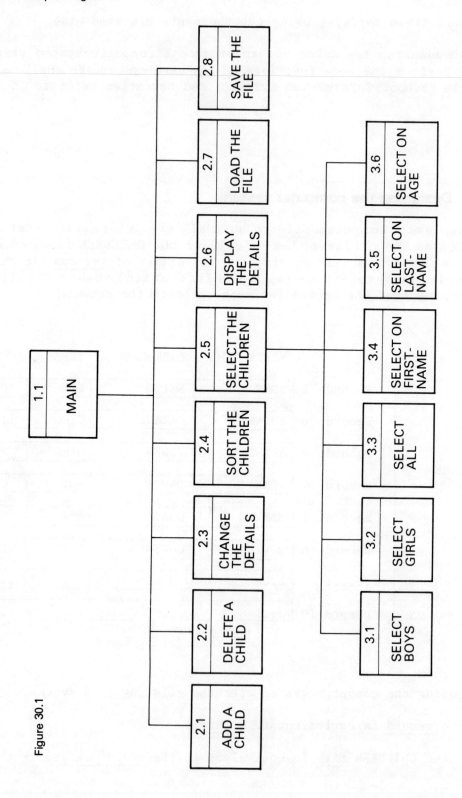

Figure 30.1

We need to carry out the same operations on the CHILDREN file as those carried out by the headmaster on his cards. In particular, we should be able to:

1. Add a child who has just joined the school.

2. Delete a child who has left the school.

3. Change the details of any child.

4. Sort the children into alphabetical order.

5. Select children according to some conditions, e.g. BOYS with an AGE of 9.

6. Display the details of selected children.

7. Load the file from cassette, when it is needed.

8. Save the file on cassette, so that it can be used again.

One approach when dealing with a large problem is to divide the problem into units of manageable size. Each unit can then be considered in turn, independently of the other units. In the context of programming, a unit is called a module. Developing programs in this way is called modular programming.

An outline of the SIS program is shown in the module chart of Figure 30.1 (a 'module chart' is sometimes called a structure chart, because it shows the structure of the program). Each box represents a module. The boxes numbered 2.1, 2.2,... 2.8 are the modules which carry out the eight tasks listed above. The purpose of the MAIN module (Module 1.1) is to determine what the headmaster wants to do next, and then to call the appropriate Level 2 module. Notice that Module 2.5 calls further modules (numbered 3.1, 3.2,... 3.6) depending on what type of selection the headmaster wants to make. The SIS module chart has a definite structure. The MAIN module is at Level 1. At Level 2 there are the eight modules (2.1, 2.2,... 2.8) which carry out the eight tasks required. The module number indicates the number of a module within a particular level (hence, 2.5 means Module 5 in Level 2). The modules called by Level 2 modules are at Level 3. If there were any modules called by Level 3 modules, they would be at Level 4; and so on.

We are going to develop our program using the top-down approach. As the name implies, we start at the top of the module chart, and develop Module 1.1. When we have a program for this module, and it has been tested to our satisfaction, then we move down the module chart, and develop a Level 2 module, for example

Module 2.7 'load the file'. The Module 1.1 program is then extended to include the commands to carry out the function of Module 2.7; indeed, we use the existing program to test the module we are developing. When it is working to our satisfaction, we then develop another Level 2 module, and add it to the existing program. And so on. Hence, we gradually build up our program by adding modules. Each is thoroughly tested before we go on to develop another.

We have chosen names to reflect what is required of the modules. Our next step is to specify in greater detail exactly what is to be done by each module. This is done in the following sections. Starting from an outline specification, we gradually add more detail to our specification until we are in a position to write it in BASIC. This is the step-wise refinement process we met in Section 13.3; we proceed in steps, refining the previous step by adding more detail, until we have sufficient detail to write the program.

30.3 The MAIN module

The basic outline of MAIN is:

```
define the arrays
repeat
     find out what the headmaster wants to do
     call the appropriate module
until finished
end
```

We now need to expand this outline by adding more detail.

30.3.1 Define the arrays

The CHILDREN file is shown in Section 30.2. Typically, the file will be read into the computer's memory from cassette, then the operations will be carried out, and finally the information will be saved back on the cassette. While in memory, the information can be held in arrays.

```
10 REM   SCHOOL INFORMATION SYSTEM   (SIS1)
20
30 DIM FIRST$(10), LAST$(10), TYPE$(10), AGE(10)
40 MAXIMUM=10
50
```

We have defined four arrays:

FIRST$ to hold the first-names of the children;
LAST$ to hold the last-names of the children;
TYPE$ to say whether a child is a BOY or a GIRL;
AGE   to hold the ages of the children.

The variable MAXIMUM is set to the number of boxes we have defined in each array. To make testing easier while developing the system, we have set MAXIMUM to a small number (10). When the system is complete, and has been thoroughly tested, we can set it to a more realistic value (perhaps 200).

30.3.2 Find out what the headmaster wants to do.

This can be expanded to:

```
clear the screen
display the heading
display the menu
repeat
     get headmaster's reply
until reply is valid
```

A menu is displayed on the screen, showing the eight tasks that SIS will perform. The headmaster is invited to type a number in the range 1-8 to choose one of these tasks.

```
 70 ..CLS
 80 ..PRINT "SCHOOL INFORMATION SYSTEM"
 90 ..PRINT "========================="
100 ..PRINT
110 ..PRINT "0 = FINISH"
120 ..PRINT "1 = ADD A CHILD"
130 ..PRINT "2 = DELETE A CHILD"
140 ..PRINT "3 = CHANGE THE DETAILS"
150 ..PRINT "4 = SORT THE CHILDREN"
160 ..PRINT "5 = SELECT CHILDREN"
170 ..PRINT "6 = DISPLAY THE DETAILS"
180 ..PRINT "7 = LOAD THE FILE"
190 ..PRINT "8 = SAVE THE FILE"
200 ..PRINT
210 ..REPEAT
220 ..   INPUT "ENTER YOUR CHOICE ",REPLY$
230 ..   REPLY$=LEFT$(REPLY$,1)
240 ..UNTIL REPLY$>="0" AND REPLY$<="8"
270 ..PRINT
280 ..INPUT "PRESS  RETURN  TO CONTINUE " WAIT$
```

If the headmaster enters a number in the range 1...8, then the corresponding task will be carried out. If he types 0, the program finishes. Any other reply is treated as an error.

Line   70   : clears the screen.
Lines   80-100 : display the heading.
Lines 110-200   : display the menu.
Lines 220-230   : ask the headmaster to make his choice by typing a number between 0 and 8. If his reply is not in the range 0-8, then the REPEAT loop made up by Lines 210 and 240 ask him to choose again.
Line 280   : causes the computer to pause, waiting for the headmaster to press the RETURN key. In the meantime, the headmaster can examine what is displayed on the screen.

30.3.3 Repeat... until finished

We can use a REPEAT loop for this, and use a reply of "0" to signify that the headmaster has finished.

```
    60 REPEAT
       ...
       ...  Lines 70-280
       ...
   290 UNTIL REPLY$="0"
   300 PRINT
   310 PRINT "EXIT FROM THE SCHOOL INFORMATION SYSTEM"
   320 END
```


PRACTICAL EXERCISES

- -

Type in the program shown in this section. List it, and check that you have typed it correctly. Now run the program, and check that it runs as shown below:

Input   Expected behaviour

0   : The program should finish with the EXIT message.
1...8   : The computer should pause waiting for you to press the RETURN key. When you do so, the menu should be redisplayed, asking you for another entry.
anything else: You should be asked again to ENTER YOUR CHOICE.

- -

When the program is working correctly, save it on your cassette as SIS1.

- -

30.3.4 Call the appropriate module

The only part of the MAIN module that now remains to be expanded is the part that calls the modules. To do this, we can make use of the ON... GOSUB command described in Section 25.3.

```
250 ..IF REPLY$="0" THEN 290
260 ..ON VAL(REPLY$) GOSUB 1000, 2000, 3000, 4000, 5000,
                          6000, 7000, 8000
```

If a reply of 0 is entered, the computer skips to Line 290 and ends the outer REPEAT loop. Otherwise, the ON... GOSUB causes:

the subroutine at Line 1000 to be called, if REPLY$ is "1"; the subroutine at Line 2000 to be called, if REPLY$ is "2"; and so on.

We need to convert the REPLY$ string to its equivalent number using the VAL function because the ON... GOSUB command requires a numeric variable following the ON. The VAL function is explained in Appendix B.

PRACTICAL EXERCISES

- -

Type in Lines 250 and 260. List the program, and check that you have typed them correctly.

- -

In order to test the program, we need to have subroutines at Lines 1000, 2000,... 8000. At this stage, we provide skeleton subroutines of the form:

```
1000
1010 CLS
1020 PRINT "ADD A CHILD"
1030 PRINT "==========="
1040 PRINT
1050 RETURN
```

```
2000
2010 CLS
2020 PRINT "DELETE A CHILD"
2030 PRINT "=============="
2040 PRINT
2050 RETURN
....
8000
8010 CLS
8020 PRINT "SAVE THE FILE"
8030 PRINT "============="
8040 PRINT
8050 RETURN
```

Type in these eight subroutines. List the program, and check that you have typed them correctly. Now run the program, and check that it performs correctly. In particular, you should enter:

1   and check that the ADD A CHILD subroutine is called;
2   and check that the DELETE A CHILD subroutine is called;
    ...
8   and check that the SAVE THE FILE subroutine is called.

- -

When the program is working correctly, save it on your cassette as SIS2.

- -

30.4 The STATUS array

We have now completed the MAIN module, and so we can progress down the module chart to a module at Level 2. Before doing so, however, we should recall that we need to be able to:

a) delete children from the information system;
b) select children according to specific conditions.

How can we keep track of children who have been deleted or selected? A simple method is to introduce another array called STATUS$, made up of 10 boxes.

If the STATUS box of a child contains an R, then that child has been Rejected with regard to the current selection condition. For example, if we were selecting BOYS, then all the GIRL entries would be rejected. In the following example, SUSAN GREAVES and ALISON JONES have been rejected, and their STATUS boxes have been set to R.

	FIRST$	LAST$	TYPE$	AGE	STATUS$
1	JOHN	,SMITH	BOY	10	S
2	SUSAN	GREAVES	GIRL	11	R
3	ALISON	JONES	GIRL	9	R
4	JOHN	DAVIS	BOY	9	F
5	MARTIN	COATS	BOY	9	S
6	DAVID	COATS	BOY	12	S
7					F
8					F
9					F
10					F

If the STATUS box contains an F (standing for F̲ree), then that entry line is available to be used when a new child is added. The STATUS box of a child who has left the school, and hence has been deleted from the system, is also set to F. In this example, JOHN DAVIS has left the school.

If the STATUS box of a child contains an S, then that child has been S̲elected with regard to the current selection condition. Hence, in this example, all the BOYS are selected, except for JOHN DAVIS who has left the school.

We will look at the STATUS array in more detail when we consider the individual modules. Most modules rely on there being CHILDREN information already in the program, and so it makes sense to begin with the module that loads data into the program.

30.5 LOAD THE FILE (Module 2.7)

In order to make more rapid progress at this early stage, we will write a skeleton LOAD THE FILE module that simply loads data from DATA commands within the program. We will of course return to the module later, and develop it to load data from your cassette.

PRACTICAL EXERCISES

- -

Type

```
35 DIM STATUS$(10)
41 FOR K=1 TO MAXIMUM
42    STATUS$(K)="F"
43 NEXT K
```

to define the STATUS array, and to set all the boxes to F.

- -

Type

```
7050 RESTORE
7060 READ NUMBER
7070 FOR K=1 TO NUMBER
7080    READ FIRST$(K),LAST$(K),TYPE$(K),AGE(K)
7090    STATUS$(K)="S"
7100 NEXT K
7110 PRINT "DATA LOADED"
7120 RETURN
7130 DATA 6
7140 DATA "JOHN", "SMITH", "BOY", 10
7150 DATA "SUSAN", "GREAVES", "GIRL", 11
7160 DATA "ALISON","JONES", "GIRL", 9
7170 DATA "JOHN", "DAVIS", "BOY", 9
7180 DATA "MARTIN", "COATS", "BOY", 9
7190 DATA "DAVID", "COATS", "BOY", 12
```

List the program, and check that you have typed it correctly.

Line 7060   accepts the value 6 from the first DATA command (Line 7130), and stores it in NUMBER. Hence, there are 6 children in the system.

Lines 7070–7100 load the first 6 boxes of the FIRST, LAST, TYPE and AGE arrays with the values contained in the six DATA commands (Lines 7140–7190).

Line 7090   sets the STATUS box for each of the six children to S (Selected).

Line 7050   If we want to LOAD THE FILE more than once, we will have to re-read the items in the DATA list. Hence, we have the RESTORE command to set the DATA list back to its original state (i.e. the 6 specified in Line 7130 becomes the first item).

Now run the program and select option 7. The message DATA LOADED should appear on the screen. At this stage, you won't be able to tell whether the data has been loaded correctly, but you will be able to when you have written the next module.

Save the program on your cassette as SIS3.

30.6 DISPLAY THE DETAILS (Module 2.6)

We want to display the details of all those children who have been selected. The details of rejected or deleted children should not appear. We can do this by displaying the details of children whose STATUS box contains an S.

Type

```
6050 FOR K=1 TO MAXIMUM
6060    IF STATUS$(K)<>"S" THEN 6080
6070    PRINT ;K,FIRST$(K),LAST$(K),TYPE$(K),AGE(K)
6080 NEXT K
6090 PRINT
6100 PRINT "DISPLAY COMPLETE"
6110 RETURN
```

List the program, and check that you have typed it correctly. Run the program and select option 7. Now select option 6 and check that it displays the details on all six children. Now select option 0 to terminate the program.

- -

Run the program and select option 6. You should find that there are no children in the system, because we haven't loaded the children. We can automatically load the children at the start of the program by including a call to the LOAD THE FILE module.

Type

```
45 GOSUB 7000          : REM  LOAD THE FILE
```

Now repeat this exercise, and check that the children are displayed correctly.

- -

When the program is working correctly, save it on your cassette as SIS4.

- -

30.7 SELECT CHILDREN (Module 2.5)

The headmaster wants to be able to:

    1. select the BOYS.
    2. select the GIRLS.
    3. select ALL the children.
    4. select children whose FIRST-NAMES satisfy some condition.
    5. select children whose LAST-NAMES satisfy some condition.
    6. select children whose AGES satisfy some condition.

Additionally, he should be able to combine the selections, for example, select BOYS whose AGE is 9. This module is similar to the MAIN module, in that it provides a 'select' menu, and asks the headmaster to enter his choice.

PRACTICAL EXERCISES

- -

Type

```
5050 PRINT "0 = FINISH"
5060 PRINT "1 = SELECT BOYS"
5070 PRINT "2 = SELECT GIRLS"
5080 PRINT "3 = SELECT ALL"
5090 PRINT "4 = SELECT ON FIRST-NAME"
5100 PRINT "5 = SELECT ON LAST-NAME"
5110 PRINT "6 = SELECT ON AGE"
5120 PRINT
5130 REPEAT
5140   INPUT "ENTER YOUR CHOICE ",ANSWER$
5150   ANSWER$=LEFT$(ANSWER$,1)
5160 UNTIL ANSWER$>="0" AND ANSWER$<="6"
5170
5180 IF ANSWER$="0" THEN RETURN
5190

5940 PRINT "STATUS = ";
5950 FOR K=1 TO MAXIMUM
5960   PRINT STATUS$(K);
5970 NEXT K
5980 PRINT
5990 RETURN
```

List the program, and check that you have typed it correctly. Now run the program and select option 5. Check that the program is working correctly. Lines 5940-5990 display the STATUS array to enable you to check that the selections made by the Level 3 modules are correct. At this stage, the STATUS array should hold SSSSSSFFFF.

- -

When the program is working correctly, save it on your cassette as SIS5.

- -

30.7.1 SELECT BOYS (Module 3.1)

We want to reject all those children whose STATUS is S, and whose TYPE is GIRL. We ignore deleted children (whose STATUS is F), and children who have been rejected by an earlier selection (whose STATUS is R).

PRACTICAL EXERCISES

- -

Type

```
5200 IF ANSWER$<>"1" THEN 5240
5210 FOR K=1 TO MAXIMUM
5220    IF STATUS$(K)="S" AND TYPE$(K)="GIRL" THEN
            STATUS$(K)="R"
5230 NEXT K
5240 REM END-IF
5250
```

List the program, and check that you have typed it correctly. Now run the program, and choose option 5 on the MAIN menu, followed by option 1 on the SELECT menu. The STATUS array should now contain SRRSSSFFFF, indicating that the second and third children (SUSAN GREAVES and ALISON JONES) have been rejected.

- -

Choose option 6 on the MAIN menu, and check that only the four boys are displayed on the screen.

- -

Choose option 7 on the MAIN menu, followed by option 6 on the MAIN menu, and check that all six children are now displayed on the screen.

- -

30.7.2 SELECT GIRLS (Module 3.2)

This module is very similar to Module 3.1, but in this case we want to reject all those children whose STATUS is S and whose TYPE is BOY.

- -

Fill in the BASIC commands for this module:

```
5300 IF ANSWER$<>"2" THEN 5340
5310 FOR K=1 TO MAXIMUM
....
....
....
5350
```

List the program, and check that you have typed it correctly. Now run the program, and choose option 5 on the MAIN menu, followed by option 2 on the SELECT menu. The STATUS aray should now contain RSSRRRFFFF, indicating that only the girls have been selected.

- -

Choose option 6 on the MAIN menu, and check that only the two girls are displayed on the screen.

- -

Choose option 5 on the MAIN menu, followed by option 1 on the SELECT menu. The STATUS array should now contain RRRRRRFFFF, indicating that all the children have been rejected. Can you explain why?

- -

Choose option 6 on the MAIN menu, and check that no children are displayed on the screen.

- -

Choose option 7 on the MAIN menu, followed by option 6 on the MAIN menu, and check that all six children are now displayed on the screen.

- -

30.7.3 SELECT ALL (Module 3.3)

This module restores the STATUS to S (Selected) of all the children who have been Rejected by previous selections.

Type
```
5400 IF ANSWER$<>"3" THEN 5440
5410 FOR K=1 TO MAXIMUM
5420   IF STATUS$(K)="R" THEN STATUS$(K)="S"
5430 NEXT K
5440 REM END-IF
5450
```

List the program, and check that you have typed it corectly. Now run the program and choose option 5 on the MAIN menu, followed by option 1 on the SELECT menu. Choose option 6 on the MAIN menu, and check that only four boys are displayed on the screen.

- -

Choose option 5 on the MAIN menu, followed by option 3 on the SELECT menu. The STATUS array should now contain SSSSSSFFFF, indicating that all the children have been selected. Now choose option 6 on the MAIN menu, and confirm that all six children are displayed on the screen.

- -

When the program is working correctly, save it on your cassette as SIS6.

- -

30.8 Review

We have now completed Modules 1.1, 2.5, 2.6, 2.7, 3.1, 3.2 and 3.3, and have established a framework for the School Information System. The complete program for these modules is shown on the following pages (it has not been renumbered so that its line-numbers correspond to the descriptions in this unit). You should now be in a position where you can build onto this framework by adding the remaining modules. Outline specifications of these modules are provided in Appendix C.

Questions

1.   What is a module?

2.   What is meant by modular programming?

3.   What is a module chart?

4.   What is meant by the term top-down?

5.   What is step-wise refinement?

6.   What advantages are there in using a top-down approach to programming?

```
 10 REM   SCHOOL INFORMATION SYSTEM   (SIS6)
 20
 30 DIM FIRST$(10), LAST$(10), TYPE$(10), AGE(10)
 35 DIM STATUS$(10)
 40 MAXIMUM=10
 41 FOR K=1 TO MAXIMUM
 42    STATUS$(K)="F"
 43 NEXT K
 45 GOSUB 7000            : REM   LOAD THE FILE
 50
 60 REPEAT
 70    CLS
 80    PRINT "SCHOOL INFORMATION SYSTEM"
 90    PRINT "========================="
100    PRINT
110    PRINT "0 = FINISH"
120    PRINT "1 = ADD A CHILD"
130    PRINT "2 = DELETE A CHILD"
140    PRINT "3 = CHANGE THE DETAILS"
150    PRINT "4 = SORT THE CHILDREN"
160    PRINT "5 = SELECT CHILDREN"
170    PRINT "6 = DISPLAY THE DETAILS"
180    PRINT "7 = LOAD THE FILE"
190    PRINT "8 = SAVE THE FILE"
200    PRINT
210    REPEAT
220      INPUT "ENTER YOUR CHOICE ",REPLY$
230      REPLY$=LEFT$(REPLY$,1)
240    UNTIL REPLY$>="0" AND REPLY$<="8"
250    IF REPLY$="0" THEN 290
260    ON VAL(REPLY$) GOSUB 1000, 2000, 3000, 4000, 5000,
                            6000, 7000, 8000
270    PRINT
280    INPUT "PRESS  RETURN  TO CONTINUE " WAIT$
290 UNTIL REPLY$="0"
300 PRINT
310 PRINT "EXIT FROM THE SCHOOL INFORMATION SYSTEM"
320 END
1000
1010 CLS
1020 PRINT "ADD A CHILD"
1030 PRINT "==========="
1040 PRINT
1050 RETURN
2000
2010 CLS
2020 PRINT "DELETE A CHILD"
2030 PRINT "=============="
2040 PRINT
```

```
2050 RETURN
3000
3010 CLS
3020 PRINT "CHANGE THE DETAILS"
3030 PRINT "=================="
3040 PRINT
3050 RETURN
4000
4010 CLS
4020 PRINT "SORT THE CHILDREN"
4030 PRINT "================="
4040 PRINT
4050 RETURN
5000
5010 CLS
5020 PRINT "SELECT CHILDREN"
5030 PRINT "==============="
5040 PRINT
5050 PRINT "0 = FINISH"
5060 PRINT "1 = SELECT BOYS"
5070 PRINT "2 = SELECT GIRLS"
5080 PRINT "3 = SELECT ALL"
5090 PRINT "4 = SELECT ON FIRST-NAME"
5100 PRINT "5 = SELECT ON LAST-NAME"
5110 PRINT "6 = SELECT ON AGE"
5120 PRINT
5130 REPEAT
5140   INPUT "ENTER YOUR CHOICE ",ANSWER$
5150   ANSWER$=LEFT$(ANSWER$,1)
5160 UNTIL ANSWER$>="0" AND ANSWER$<="6"
5170
5180 IF ANSWER$="0" THEN RETURN
5190
5200 IF ANSWER$<>"1" THEN 5240
5210 FOR K=1 TO MAXIMUM
5220   IF STATUS$(K)="S" AND TYPE$(K)="GIRL" THEN
        STATUS$(K)="R"
5230 NEXT K
5240 REM END-IF
5250
5300 IF ANSWER$<>"2" THEN 5340
5310 FOR K=1 TO MAXIMUM
5320   IF STATUS$(K)="S" AND TYPE$(K)="BOY" THEN
        STATUS$(K)="R"
5330 NEXT K
5340 REM END-IF
5350
5400 IF ANSWER$<>"3" THEN 5440
5410 FOR K=1 TO MAXIMUM
```

```
5420   IF STATUS$(K)="R" THEN STATUS$(K)="S"
5430 NEXT K
5440 REM END-IF
5450
5940 PRINT "STATUS = ";
5950 FOR K=1 TO MAXIMUM
5960   PRINT STATUS$(K);
5970 NEXT K
5980 PRINT
5990 RETURN
6000
6010 CLS
6020 PRINT "DISPLAY THE DETAILS"
6030 PRINT "===================="
6040 PRINT
6050 FOR K=1 TO MAXIMUM
6060   IF STATUS$(K)<>"S" THEN 6080
6070   PRINT ;K,FIRST$(K),LAST$(K),TYPE$(K),AGE(K)
6080 NEXT K
6090 PRINT
6100 PRINT "DISPLAY COMPLETE"
6110 RETURN
7000
7010 CLS
7020 PRINT "LOAD THE FILE"
7030 PRINT "============="
7040 PRINT
7050 RESTORE
7060 READ NUMBER
7070 FOR K=1 TO NUMBER
7080   READ FIRST$(K),LAST$(K),TYPE$(K),AGE(K)
7090   STATUS$(K)="S"
7100 NEXT K
7110 PRINT "DATA LOADED"
7120 RETURN
7130 DATA 6
7140 DATA "JOHN", "SMITH", "BOY", 10
7150 DATA "SUSAN", "GREAVES", "GIRL", 11
7160 DATA "ALISON","JONES", "GIRL", 9
7170 DATA "JOHN", "DAVIS", "BOY", 9
7180 DATA "MARTIN", "COATS", "BOY", 9
7190 DATA "DAVID", "COATS", "BOY", 12
8000
8010 CLS
8020 PRINT "SAVE THE FILE"
8030 PRINT "============="
8040 PRINT
8050 RETURN
```

31 Odds and ends

31.1 Terminating a program

The END command tells the computer to finish executing the program. Up to now we have used it as the final command of a program. In fact there can be several END commands in a program, and the computer will terminate when it executes any one of them. For example, the command

        200 IF REPLY$="QUIT" THEN END

will terminate the program if REPLY$ holds the string "QUIT".

The STOP command will also terminate the execution of a program. It has the same effect as the END command, with the addition that a message is displayed on the screen stating the line-number at which execution ceased. For example, if Line 35 contains a STOP command, then the message 'STOP at line 35' will be displayed when the command is executed. This can be useful when debugging a program, because you can now:

1.   display the contents of variables, using PRINT commands (with no line-numbers);

2.   change the values of variables, using LET commands (with no line-numbers);

3.   restart the program by typing GOTO n, where n is the line-number of the line immediately following the one containing the STOP command (e.g. GOTO 40).

31.2 The GOTO command

The command 'GOTO n' causes the computer to jump to Line n. It is very tempting to use GOTO commands in your programs because they appear to be so easy to understand. However, it is well known that GOTO's actually make programs more difficult to follow. This is particularly the case as your programs become larger. This book has used the GOTO command very sparingly, and you are encouraged to do likewise. Whenever you are tempted to use a GOTO, stop and think carefully about whether there is an alternative. In particular, do not use a GOTO to produce a loop (REPEAT loops or FOR loops are much easier to understand). In general, a GOTO should only be used to make an early exit from a sequence of commands.

31.3 The IF... THEN... ELSE command

In Unit 10, we saw IF commands of the form:

```
10 IF X=1 THEN PRINT "HEADS" :
              ADDUP1=ADDUP1+1
         ELSE PRINT "TAILS" :
              ADDUP2=ADDUP2+1
```

where there were two commands separated by a colon on the THEN branch (PRINT "HEADS" and ADDUP1=ADDUP1+1), and two commands separated by a colon on the ELSE branch (PRINT "TAILS" and ADDUP2=ADDUP2+1). This has to be typed into the computer as one long line. Sometimes your IF command will be too long to fit onto one BASIC line (238 characters is the maximum length). We can overcome this problem by using the following construct:

```
10 IF X=1 THEN 50
20    PRINT "TAILS"
30    ADDUP2=ADDUP2+1
40 GOTO 70
50    PRINT "HEADS"
60    ADDUP1=ADDUP1+1
70 REM END-IF
```

If the condition in Line 10 is true, then Lines 50 and 60 (the THEN branch) are executed. If the condition is false, then Lines 20 and 30 (the ELSE branch) are executed. Any number of commands may now be included on the THEN branch or the ELSE branch. They are indented in the usual way. An example of this construct is shown in Lines 1200-1290 of Example Program II, on Page 196.

31.4 Saving memory space

Sometimes your program becomes too large to fit into the computer's memory. What can you do when this happens? Throughout this book you have been encouraged to include explanatory remarks in your program, to make the purpose of the commands clearer. These remarks actually take up quite a lot of memory, so the simplest way to reduce the space required by your program is to eliminate these remarks. If you arrive at the situation of your program not fitting in memory, then you may not have any alternative but to cut down on your remarks. Before doing so, however, make sure that you keep notes on how the program works, otherwise you may have difficulty understanding it, especially if you decide to modify it in a few months time.

You can also save memory space by putting several commands on one line rather than having them as separate lines of the program. The disadvantage of doing this, however, is that your programs again become harder to read.

BBC BASIC allows you to specify that a variable will hold only whole numbers. This is done by including a % at the end of the name, for example K%. These are called <u>integer variables</u>. They are commonly used as subscripts for arrays, or as loop control variables. For example:

```
10 FOR K%=1 TO 10
20    PRINT ADDUP(K%)
30 NEXT K%
```

Integer variables take less space in memory than ordinary number variables, and so you can make some saving in memory space by using them.

Execution is faster when integer variables are used. For example, a FOR loop executes more quickly with an integer loop-control variable.

Type
```
10 TIME=0
20 FOR K%=1 TO 10000 : NEXT
30 PRINT TIME/100
40 END
```

and run the program. Now change K% in Line 20 to K, and rerun the program. Notice how much longer the loop now takes to execute.

31.5 User-friendly programs

Most of the programs that you have written from this book have been for your own use. Because you wrote the programs, you know:

1. the purpose of the program, and how to use it;
2. the structure of the program, and how it works;
3. what input is required, and its precise format;
4. what the output means.

This knowledge makes it simple for YOU to run a program, and to recover if you should happen to make a mistake (typing incorrect input, for example). Other people, however, will find it much more difficult to run these programs, simply because they don't have this knowledge. Consequently, when you are writing programs for other people to use, you should:

1.   Explain the purpose of the program. This should be written on paper (so that the user can read it before running the program). It should also appear on the screen when the user commences running the program.

2.   Explain how to run the program. Again, the explanation should be both on paper and on the screen. You need to explain which keys the user can press, and their function.

3.   Keep the user informed as to what to do next. For example, if the program wants the number of the next runner entered, then display a message on the screen, such as 'PLEASE ENTER NUMBER OF RUNNER'.

4.   Ensure that your program checks that every entry made by the user is valid. For example, if the runner number must be between 1 and 15, then the program should reject entries such as 1A, 210, at the same time informing the user that his entry is incorrect.

5.   Ensure that the user's typing mistakes cannot cause your program to go wrong.

31.6 What now?

If you have got to this point and have successfully completed all the Units in the book, then you are to be congratulated. The question arises as to what you can do now. Here are some possibilities:

Perhaps you might like to learn how a computer actually works internally. One way to achieve this is to learn to program it in what is called 'assembly language'. There are a number of books available which describe the assembly language of the BBC computer.

Perhaps you might like to become more proficient in programming. One way to do this is to purchase an advanced book on programming, for example 'Software Engineering for small computers' by R. B. Coats, published by Edward Arnold. This book describes further programming techniques, and is aimed at people such as youself who have grasped the rudiments of programming.

Appendix A—Answers

Unit 3: Question 11

```
10 LET SPEED=60
20 PRINT SPEED
30 LET HOURS=4
40 PRINT HOURS
50 LET MILES=SPEED*HOURS
60 PRINT MILES
70 END
```

Unit 4: Questions 8 and 9

```
10 INPUT "ENTER AGE ",AGE
15 INPUT "ENTER WEEKLY AMOUNT ",WEEKLY
20 LET PAY=WEEKLY*AGE
30 PRINT "POCKET MONEY = ";PAY;" PENCE PER WEEK"
40 END
```

Unit 7: Question 8

```
10 BILL=0
20 REPEAT
30    INPUT "ENTER ITEM ",ITEM
40    BILL=BILL+ITEM
50 UNTIL ITEM=0
60 PRINT
70 PRINT "TOTAL BILL = ";BILL
80 END
```

Unit 8: Question 10

1. A FOR command with no corresponding NEXT command;
2. a NEXT command with no corresponding FOR command;
3. the name in the NEXT command isn't the same as the name in the FOR command;
4. a STEP value of 0 is used.

Unit 9: Question 2

```
10 FOR K=1 TO 20
20   X=RND(2)
30   PRINT X
40 NEXT K
50 END
```


Unit 10: Question 5

Line 40, because A+B is NOT greater than 25 - it is actually
equal to 25. Hence, the condition is FALSE.

Unit 10: Question 6

```
10 REM  FOOTBALL RESULTS  (FOOTBALL1)
20
30 REPEAT
40   INPUT "HOME TEAM GOALS ",HOME
50   INPUT "VISITORS  GOALS ",VISITORS
60
70   IF HOME>VISITORS THEN PRINT "HOME WIN"
80   IF HOME<VISITORS THEN PRINT "AWAY WIN"
90   IF HOME=VISITORS THEN PRINT "DRAW"
100   PRINT
110 UNTIL HOME<0
120 END
```


Unit 11: Question 5

DIM MONTH(12). This command actually defines 13 boxes,
numbered 0, 1, 2,... 12, but we ignore Box 0 in this book.

Unit 12: Question 1

a)   200 DIM POSITION(15),CNT(15),USED(15)

b)   995 ..USED(RUNNER)=1

c)   930 ..IF USED(RUNNER)=1 THEN
                PRINT "NUMBER ALREADY USED" :
                GOTO 700
      935 ..

Unit 13: Question 6

```
10 REM   CROSS-COUNTRY PROGRAM   (CROSS3)
20 DIM CNT(3)
30
40 REM   READ THE RESULTS / CALCULATE THE TEAM TOTALS
50
60 FOR K=1 TO 15
70    PRINT
80    PRINT "POSITION ";K;
90    INPUT "  RUNNER ",RUNNER
100   TEAM=1 + (RUNNER-1) DIV 5
110   CNT(TEAM)=CNT(TEAM)+K
120 NEXT K
130 PRINT
140
150 REM   DISPLAY THE RESULTS
160
170 FOR TEAM=1 TO 3
180   PRINT "TEAM ";TEAM;"   ";CNT(TEAM)
190 NEXT TEAM
200
210 END
```

Unit 13: Question 7

```
10 REM   BIRTHDAY HISTOGRAMS   (BIRTHDAY1)
20 DIM ADDUP(12)
30
40 INPUT "ENTER NUMBER OF CHILDREN ",NUMBER
50 IF NUMBER<1  THEN PRINT "TOO SMALL" : GOTO 40
60 IF NUMBER>30 THEN PRINT "TOO LARGE" : GOTO 40
70 PRINT
80
90 REM   GET THE BIRTHDAY MONTHS
100
110 FOR K=1 TO NUMBER
120   PRINT "CHILD ";K;
130   INPUT "  BIRTHDAY MONTH = ",MONTH
140   IF MONTH<1  THEN PRINT "TOO SMALL" : GOTO 120
150   IF MONTH>12 THEN PRINT "TOO LARGE" : GOTO 120
160   ADDUP(MONTH)=ADDUP(MONTH)+1
170 NEXT K
180 PRINT
190
200 REM   DISPLAY THE HISTOGRAM
210
```

```
220 FOR A1=1 TO 12
230    PRINT A1;"   ";
240    IF ADDUP(A1)=0 THEN 280
250    FOR J=1 TO ADDUP(A1)
260       PRINT "*";
270    NEXT J
280    PRINT
290 NEXT A1
300
310 END
```

Unit 14: Question 7

```
45 ..IF TABLE=0 THEN 100
```

Unit 15: Question 10

    a)   A$=LEFT$(B$,4)
    b)   A$=RIGHT$(B$,4)
    c)   A$=MID$(B$,1,4)
    d)   A$=MID$(B$, LEN(B$)-3, 4)

Unit 15: Question 12

Strictly speaking, the FOR loop between Lines 160 and 180 should not be executed at all when USED$ contains a null string. As the program stands, it will be executed ONCE, simply because a FOR loop is always executed at least once. It does not cause any harm, however, because the condition in Line 170 will not be satisfied, and so the computer will proceed to Line 190 correctly.

Unit 17: Question 10

The program is the same as the program described in Section 17.3, except that you should:

    1.   replace TABLE$ by TABLE;
    2.   replace SMALLEST$ by SMALLEST;
    3.   replace "ZZZZZZZZ" by 99999999;
    4.   change Line 210 to   DATA 9
    5.   change Line 220 to   DATA 21,17,3,97,84,27,11,9,21
    6.   delete Line 230;

Unit 17: Question 11

```
10 INPUT "ENTER STRING ",A$
20
30 B$=""
40 IF A$="" THEN 110
50 FOR K=1 TO LEN(A$)
60    N=ASC(MID$(A$,K,1))
70    IF N>=97 AND N<=122 THEN N=N-32
80    B$=B$+CHR$(N)
90 NEXT K
100
110 PRINT "NEW STRING  = ";B$
120 END
```

Lines 50-90 make up a FOR loop which:

a)   extracts each character in turn from A$, and works out its ASCII value (Line 60);

b)   if the character is a small letter (i.e. it has an ASCII value between 97 and 122), converts it to a capital letter by subtracting 32 from its ASCII value (Line 70);

c)   concatenates the character to B$ (Line 80). Hence, by the end of the loop, B$ contains the same characters as A$, but with small letters converted to capitals.

Note: AND is explained in Unit 18, but its meaning here is obvious.

Unit 18: Question 1

a)   1 2 3 4 6 7 8

b)   5 6 7 8

c)   3 4 5 6 7

d)   none - it is impossible for K to be less than 2 <u>and</u> greater than 6 <u>at the same time</u>.

Unit 23: Question 13

Add the following lines to the 'bouncing #' program:

```
41 MINROW=5 : MAXROW=15

60 FOR ROW=MINROW TO MAXROW

81
82 FOR COL=MINCOL TO MAXCOL
83    PRINT TAB(COL,MINROW-1);"-";
84    PRINT TAB(COL,MAXROW+1);"-";
85 NEXT COL

111 ADDTOROW=1

191
192 ..ROW=ROW+ADDTOROW
193 ..IF ROW=MINROW OR ROW=MAXROW THEN ADDTOROW=-ADDTOROW
```

Unit 26: Question 9

```
OUTSIDE  K = 1
INSIDE   K = 1
INSIDE   K = 2
INSIDE   K = 3
FINISHED
```

The value of K is changed within PROC_EXAMPLE. When Line 40 is reached, K has a value of 4, which terminates the FOR loop in Lines 10-40 after only ONE execution of the loop.

Unit 29: Question 6

```
Test case        : 1
Purpose          : to test for a HOME WIN
Test data        : HOME = 5, VISITORS = 2
Expected result  : HOME WIN should be displayed

Test case        : 2
Purpose          : to test for an AWAY WIN
Test data        : HOME = 0, VISITORS = 3
Expected result  : AWAY WIN should be displayed
```

Test case   : 3
Purpose   : to test for a DRAW
Test data   : HOME = 2, VISITORS = 2
Expected result   : DRAW should be displayed

Test case   : 4
Purpose   : to test that the program terminates
Test data   : HOME = -1, VISITORS = 2
Expected result   : the program should terminate

Unit 29: Question 9

```
45 ..IF HOME<0 THEN 120
```

Appendix B—Summary of BASIC

ABS(K)   absolute value of K. This function makes a 'minus' number into a 'plus' number, but leaves a 'plus' number as it is. For example ABS(-3.5) is equal to 3.5; ABS(3.5) is equal to 3.5.

ACS(K)   arc-cosine. This function returns the angle (in radians) whose cosine is K.

AND   ensures that both of two conditions are met before something is done. E.g. IF AGE>10 AND AGE<15 THEN...

ASC(X$)   ASCII. This function returns the ASCII code of the first character of X$. The ASCII code of "A", for example, is 65.

ASN(K)   arc-sine. This function returns the angle (in radians) whose sine is K.

ATN(K)   arc-tangent. This function returns the angle (in radians) whose tangent is K.

AUTO   automatic. The computer automatically generates line-numbers when you are typing in a program. Pressing the ESCAPE key terminates the automatic numbering.

CHR$(K)   character. This function returns the character whose ASCII code is K. For example, CHR$(65) is "A".

CLG   clear the graphics screen. The graphics area of the screen is cleared, and left in the current graphics background colour.

CLOSE#F1   tells the computer to close the file assigned to F1.

CLS   clear the text screen. The text area of the screen is cleared, and left in the current text background colour.

COLOUR   selects the foreground and background colour in which the computer will print text.

COS(K)   cosine. This function returns the cosine of K, where K is in radians.

DATA   stores numeric and string data items within the program itself, for use by the READ command.

DEF   define. This command is used to define procedures and user-defined functions. For example, DEF PROC_SHOOT.

DEG(K)   degrees. This function converts the angle K (expressed in radians) into degrees.

DELETE   this command is used to delete a group of lines from a program.

DIM   dimension of an array. This command is used to declare an array within a program. For example, DIM ADDUP(6).

DIV   division of whole numbers. This gives the whole number part of the result of a division. For example, 7 DIV 2 is equal to 3.

DRAW   this command draws lines on the screen. It can be used in graphics Modes 0, 1, 2, 4, and 5.

ELSE   is part of the 'IF condition THEN... ELSE...' command. The commands on the ELSE branch are executed when the condition is FALSE. An ELSE can also be used with the 'ON... GOSUB' command, e.g. ON... GOSUB... ELSE.

END   tells the computer that it has reached the end of the program.

ENDPROC   marks the end of a procedure.

ENVELOPE   this command controls the loudness and pitch of a sound while it is being played. It is used in conjunction with the SOUND command.

EOF#F1   has the value TRUE if the end of the file assigned to F1 has been reached.

EXP(K)   exponent. This function returns the value 2.7183... (e) raised to the power of K.

FN   function. FN attached to a variable name indicates a user-defined function. E.g. FN_CALCULATE_PAY(AGE).

FOR   marks the start of a FOR... NEXT loop.

GCOL   graphics colour. This command is used to select the foreground and background colours in which the computer will perform graphics.

GET$ this function waits for a key to be pressed. The character of the pressed key is returned by the function. The computer does not wait for the RETURN key to be pressed.

GOSUB n   go to a subroutine. This command is used to call the subroutine at Line n. A RETURN command in the subroutine causes the computer to return to the line immediately following the GOSUB command.

GOTO n   go to a line-number. This command causes the computer to jump to Line n.

IF   is part of the 'IF condition THEN... ELSE...' command. It creates a test condition which controls what the computer will do next.

INKEY$ input the character pressed. This function causes the computer to wait for a specified length of time. If a key is pressed in this time, the function returns the character corresponding to that key. Otherwise it returns a null string. The computer then continues.

INPUT   accepts information typed at the keyboard, and stores it in the computer's memory, for use by the program.

INPUT#   accepts information from a file on cassette, and stores it in the computer's memory, for use by the program.

INSTR   in string. This function searches one string for any occurrence of another string. The number returned by the function is the position of the first occurrence of the string. For example, INSTR("ABCDE","CD") will return 3, because "CD" occurs in "ABCDE" at position 3.

INT   integer part. This function returns the whole number part of a number, e.g. INT(3.75) is equal to 3.

LEFT$ this function returns the left-hand part of a string.
           For example, LEFT$("ABCDE",3) will return the three
           characters at the left-hand end of "ABCDE", i.e. "ABC".

LEN(A$)   length. This function returns the number of characters
           in a string. For example, LEN("ABCDE") is equal to 5.

LET   is an optional part of an assignment command. LET AGE=9
           can be abbreviated to AGE=9.

LIST   causes the program stored in the computer's memory to
           be displayed on the screen.

LN(K)   natural logarithm. This function returns the natural
           logarithm of K.

LOAD   causes a program to be loaded from cassette into the
           computer's memory.

LOCAL K   tells the computer that K is local to the procedure or
           function containing the command.

LOG(K)   logarithm. This function returns the logarithm of K, to
           the base 10.

MID$ this function extracts a substring from a string. For
           example, MID$("ABCDE",2,3) returns the 3-character
           string beginning at the 2nd character position of
           "ABCDE", namely "BCD".

MOD   modulus. This gives the remainder after division. For
           example, 7 MOD 2 is equal to 1.

MODE K   sets the graphics mode to K (0-7).

MOVE   this command moves the graphics cursor to some
           specified point on the screen.

NEW   this command removes the program currently in the
           computer's memory.

NEXT   marks the end of a FOR... NEXT loop.

NOT   is used to reverse the effect of some test. For
           example, IF NOT (AGE=10) THEN...

OLD   this command recovers a program after NEW has been
           entered, or the BREAK key pressed.

ON   is used in conjunction with the GOSUB command, to provide multi-way switching. E.g. ON K GOSUB 10,20,30.

OPENIN   opens a file for input. The computer will read values from the cassette, and store them in memory.

OPENOUT   opens a file for output. Values created by a program in memory are written onto cassette.

OR   is used to ensure that something will be done when either of two conditions are met. For example, IF AGE=7 OR AGE=9 THEN...

PI   has the constant value of 3.14159265.

PLOT   is a multi-purpose command for drawing points, lines or triangles on the screen.

POINT   this function is used to find the colour at some specified point on the screen.

PRINT   displays strings and numbers on the screen.

PRINT#   this command writes strings and numbers on cassette.

PROC   procedure. PROC attached to a variable name indicates a procedure. For example, PROC_PAUSE(DELAY).

RAD(K)   radian. This function converts the angle K (expressed in degrees) into radians.

READ   this command tells the computer to read values from DATA commands, and assign these values to variables.

REM   REMark. This command causes the computer to ignore the rest of a line. The REM command enables you to put comments into a program to explain how it works.

RENUMBER   this command causes the lines of a program to be renumbered. Normally, line-numbering begins at 10, and increases in steps of 10.

REPEAT   marks the start of a REPEAT... UNTIL loop.

RESTORE   this command resets the computer so that it will READ data from the first DATA command in the program, even though this item may have been read already.

RETURN   this command marks the end of the execution of a
             subroutine. It causes the computer to return to the
             line immediately following the GOSUB command which
             called the subroutine. More than one RETURN may be
             present in a subroutine.

RIGHT$ this function returns the right-hand part of a string.
             For example, RIGHT$("ABCDE",3) will return "CDE", the
             three characters at the right-hand end of "ABCDE".

RND(K)   random. This function returns a number generated at
             random between 1 and K

RUN   causes the computer to execute the program in memory.

SAVE   this command causes the program currently in memory to
             be saved on cassette.

SGN(K)   determines whether a number is greater than 0, equal to
             0, or less than 0. SGN(K) returns a value of:

                 +1 if K is greater than 0;
                  0 if K is equal to 0;
                 -1 if K is less than 0.

SIN(K)   sine. This function returns the sine of K, where K is
             in radians.

SOUND   causes the computer to emit sounds.

SQR(K)   square root. This function gives the square root of K.

STEP   is the part of the FOR command which specifies the size
             of the step to be added to the loop-control-variable
             each time the loop is executed.

STOP   stops the execution of the program. It has the same
             effect as END, except that a message is displayed on
             the screen showing the line-number at which the program
             stopped.

STR$ string. This function converts a number into the
             equivalent string representation. For example STR$(7.3)
             is equal to "7.3".

TAB   tabulation. This function is used with the PRINT
             command to move the cursor to specified positions on
             the screen.

TAN   <u>tangent</u>. This function returns the tangent of K, where
             K is in radians.

THEN   is part of the 'IF condition THEN... ELSE... command'.
             The commands on the THEN branch are executed if the
             condition is TRUE.

TIME   is used to read or set the computer's electronic clock.

TO   is the part of the FOR command which specifies the
             upper limit of the loop-control-variable. The loop will
             terminate when the loop-control-variable exceeds this
             upper limit.

TRACE   makes the computer display the line-number of each
             line of the program just before it is executed.

UNTIL   marks the end of a REPEAT... UNTIL loop

VAL   <u>value</u>. This function returns the numeric value of a
             string. For example, VAL("7.3") is equal to 7.3.

Appendix C—Project

A framework for the School Information System was established in Unit 30. The purpose of this project is to enlarge this framework by adding the missing modules, and, by doing so, give you some further practice at programming.

When an exercise asks you to 'write' a module, it really means design, construct, test and debug that module. The specifications provided here are only outline specifications, and you will find that more detail must be provided before you can actually code the module in BASIC.

C.1 SAVE THE FILE (Module 2.8)

Write the module to save the children information in a cassette file called CHILDREN. Add the module to the existing SIS program. See Unit 28 for a description of saving information on cassettes.

C.2 LOAD THE FILE (Module 2.7)

Write the module to load the children information into the SIS program from the CHILDREN file on your cassette. Add the module to the existing SIS program. See Unit 28 for a description of loading information from cassettes.

C.3 SORT THE CHILDREN (Module 2.4)

Write the module to sort the children into alphabetical order of LAST-NAME. Add the module to the existing SIS program. See Unit 17 for a description of sorting.

C.4 ADD A CHILD (Module 2.1)

Write the module which allows the headmaster to add the details of a new child. Add the module to the existing SIS program. An outline specification of the module follows:

```
      if NUMBER=MAXIMUM then
           print 'error - no room for more children'
           return

      for K=1 to MAXIMUM
           if STATUS$(K)="F" then free=K : K=MAXIMUM
      next K

      ask headmaster for first-name  - store it in FIRST$(free)
      ask headmaster for last-name   - store it in LAST$(free)
      ask headmaster for boy or girl - store it in TYPE$(free)
      ask headmaster for age         - store it in AGE(free)
      STATUS$(free)="S"
      NUMBER=NUMBER+1
      return
```

C.5 DELETE A CHILD (Module 2.2)

Write the module which allows the headmaster to delete a child.
Add the module to the existing SIS program. An outline of the
module follows:

```
      if NUMBER=0 then
           print 'error - no children in the system'
           return
      display-details
      ask headmaster to enter the number of the child to be
           deleted : store it in K
      STATUS$(K)="F"
      NUMBER=NUMBER-1
      return
```

The underlining of 'display-details' means another module (Module
2.6) is called to display the details of the children.

C.6 CHANGE THE DETAILS (Module 2.3)

Write the module which allows the headmaster to change the
details of a child. Add the module to the existing SIS program.
An outline specification of the module follows:

```
if NUMBER=0 then
     print 'error - no children in the system'
     return
display-details
ask the headmaster to enter the number of the child to be
     changed : store it in K
ask the headmaster if he wants to change the first-name
if yes then
     ask the headmaster to enter the new first-name
     store it in FIRST$(K)
ask the headmaster if he wants to change the last-name
if yes then
     ask the headmaster to enter the new last-name
     store it in LAST$(K)
ask the headmaster if he wants to change the type
if yes then
     ask the headmaster to enter the new type
     store it in TYPE$(K)
ask the headmaster if he wants to change the age
if yes then
     ask the headmaster to enter the new age
     store it in AGE(K)
return
```

C.7 SELECT ON FIRST-NAME (Module 3.4)

Write the module which allows the headmaster to select children
whose first-names satisfy some condition. For example, he might
want all children called JOHN. Only children whose status is S
are eligible for selection. An outline specification follows:

```
get-the-condition
ask the headmaster to enter item to be matched (e.g. "JOHN")
store it in match-item
for K=1 to MAXIMUM
     if STATUS$(K)<>"S" then
          goto <<label>>
     if condition=1 (less than) and FIRST$(K)>=match-item
          STATUS$(K)="R"
     if condition=2 (equal to) and FIRST$(K)<>match-item
          STATUS$(K)="R"
     if condition=3 (greater than) and FIRST$(K)<=match-item
          STATUS$(K)="R"
     <<label>>
next K
return
```

The 'get-the-condition' module asks the headmaster to enter the condition that is to be applied to the selection. An outline specification of the module follows:

Module : get-the-condition

```
    print "0 = finish"
    print "1 = less than"
    print "2 = equal to"
    print "3 = greater than"
    print
    repeat
        input "enter your choice ", condition
    until condition>=0 and condition<=3
    return
```

C.8 SELECT ON LAST-NAME (Module 3.5)

Write the module which allows the headmaster to select children whose last-names satisfy some condition. For example, he might want all children whose names comes after M in the alphabet, in which case he would select 'greater than M'. Only children whose status is S are eligible for selection. This module is similar to the previous one, except that LAST$ is used in place of FIRST$.

C.9 SELECT ON AGE (Module 3.6)

Write the module which allows the headmaster to select children whose ages satisfy some condition. For example, he might want all children aged nine. Only children whose status is S are eligible for selection. This module is similar to Module 3.4, except that AGE is used in place of FIRST$, and match-item is numeric rather than a string.

If the headmaster wants to select BOYS who are 9 years old, he can:

1.   run Module 3.1 to select BOYS;

2.   then run Module 3.6 (with a condition of 'equal to' and a match-item of 9) to select those boys who are aged 9.

Index